Praise for *Beyond Potential*

"*Beyond Potential* is a breath of fresh air for the accomplished but exhausted creative. Kate's approach to career reinvention is rooted in both compassion and a deep understanding of the artistic journey."

— Miriam Landis, dancer, and author of *Girl on Pointe*,
and *Lauren in the Limelight*

"With *Beyond Potential*, Kate Kayaian has taken her lived experience as a professional creative, distilled it into potent wisdom, woven it with relatable stories, and translated it into exercises and action steps that will allow your 'present self' to transform into your 'ideal self.' A powerful book for mid-career artists seeking a fresh, focused perspective and a clear path forward."

— Susan Blackwell, broadway and screen actress, writer,
director, and host of *The Spark File* podcast

"As an artist, it's easy to get lost in the pursuit of success. ***Beyond Potential*** reminds us to pause, assess, and build a career that aligns with our values and passions."

— Jennet Ingle, oboeist, and author of *The Happiest Musician*

"Kate brings wisdom and empathy to the unique challenges artists face today. ***Beyond Potential*** offers a roadmap for rediscovering joy and purpose in both career and life."

— Jennifer Rosenfeld, Broadway composer, and author of *Awakening Your Business Brain: An iCadenza Guide to Launching Your Music Career*

"An invaluable resource for mid-career creatives. Kate has a gift for distilling complex emotions into actionable advice, perfect for anyone who feels caught between career pressures and personal aspirations."

— Renée-Paule Gauthier, violinist, and host of the Mind Over Finger podcast

BEYOND POTENTIAL

A Guide for Creatives Who Want to Re-Assess,
Re-Define, and Re-Ignite Their Careers

KATE KAYAIAN

Moongate Press
655 Center St., Ste. 300095
Jamaica Plain, MA 02130

Book Cover and Interior Design by Monkey C Media

First Edition
Printed in the United States of America

ISBN:
979-8-9918782-0-3 (trade paperback)
979-8-9918782-1-0 (epub)

Library of Congress Control Number: 2024926435

I wrote this book for You.
Past You,
Present You,
and Future You.

Contents

THREE: Re-Ignite
Everything You Need to Make it Happen.................... 122

Introduction

Dear Reader,

I see you. Trying. Striving. Wondering if you're *doing it right*. Questioning whether you're on the right path and maybe it's just hard right now, or if maybe you were meant to be doing something entirely different. After all these years of effort, having achieved what most people would consider capital S "Success," you're still not feeling the sense of fulfillment you thought would come. Why not? What now?

You've dedicated a lifetime to chasing that elusive *potential* that everyone told you was out there waiting for you—a version of potential that felt exciting, glamorous, and worthy of all the long hours you spent perfecting your craft. But here you are. Perhaps you've reached it, and it didn't feel all that great. Or maybe you haven't quite reached it yet, and oddly, it doesn't bother you as much as you think it should. Or you've reached it; it was fine … but now what?

You're in that space between "young and unformed" and "too old to matter"—what used to be called a midlife crisis—except now, it's not really midlife, is it? We live longer, fuller lives. Just as a young professional ballet dancer knows they are likely to have a second career when they retire from the stage in their thirties, these days, a fifty-year-old accountant can also start anew. So can a sixty-year-old lawyer or a forty-five-year-old pianist.

The world is more open than ever to second beginnings.

And this isn't a crisis. Not really. You could continue on your current path just fine. Plenty of others like you have done just that. But instead, you're standing at a threshold, feeling a spark of energy and curiosity. Something inside of you is stirring quietly, but persistently asking: "What else?"

You're not starting out anymore, nor are you ready to pack it in. You've gained experience, honed your skills, and gotten to know yourself (a bit more, anyway). Most importantly, you have time— more than you realize.

So now you're asking, "If I have this one life, and the wisdom to choose how I spend it, what would my best-lived life look like?" It's not the life you chose twenty or thirty years ago—it's the life you'd choose today. What if you lived out your deepest, most secret dreams, achieved the goals you've never told anyone about?

What would it feel like to break free from the outdated definitions of "potential" handed to you by others—teachers, parents, childhood dreams—and instead, live your truest, most aligned, most fulfilling life?

There's a story that when you arrive in heaven, you aren't greeted by Saint Peter, but by the version of yourself who did all the things you truly wanted to do—the version that went beyond your accepted potential and found your truth. Your Beyond Potential Self.

You know that version of yourself, don't you? The one who speaks fluent Spanish, has traveled the world, or mastered the perfect chocolate soufflé. The version that has the dream career filled with purpose and passion, the vibrant relationships, and a home that looks like those houses in magazines. The one who's invested wisely—not just in stocks, but in themself. The one who has lived *fully*.

But how do you get there? How do you figure out what still matters and what doesn't? What if you've wandered so off course that you can't find your way back? And once you know what it is you want, where you want to be, where do you even begin?

What if you could stand at the end of your days, look that ideal version of yourself in the eyes, and realize you're one and the same?

That's why I wrote this book.

Inside, I'll guide you through the process I've used with myself and creatives like you from all around the world—musicians, actors, painters, dancers, sculptors, and also creative people in very *un*-creative jobs looking to bust out of their shell and become who they were meant to be. Part of that process is in laying out helpful frameworks, strategies, and ideas, and part of it involves written exercises that I think you will find hugely beneficial—especially the ones you might have an initial resistance to! Both parts of this process will help you to look at your past, present, and future in new and fresh ways.

Throughout the book, I intentionally set apart the prefix "re-" ("again" or "anew") to remind you of this fresh-eyed evaluation of our lives and our stories. In these pages, we'll *re*-assess, *re*-define, and *re*-ignite your career—and your life.

Are you ready? Let's begin.

ONE

Re-Assess

Where Are You and How Did You Get Here?

1

Re-Assessing Your Inner Programming

You are braver than you believe, stronger than you seem, and smarter than you think.

– A.A. Milne

I heard a story several years ago about a kindergarten teacher who asked her young students to draw a picture of what they wanted to be when they grew up. With crayons and paper, the kids excitedly began sketching out visual representations of their biggest dreams in the way only a future Spider-Man or president can. Most of the children drew doctors, lawyers, ballet dancers, and firefighters—the usual suspects in a five-year-old's imaginative dreamscape.

But the teacher grew concerned about one boy, new to the school, who drew a picture of a man in a baseball cap, carrying a pizza box.

Worried, she called the boy's mother to understand the drawing. After a deep exhale, the mother explained: the boy's father was in prison; his older brother had died from a drug overdose; and several of his cousins were involved in gangs. However, the boy had one cousin, James, who was different. James had stayed clean, avoided drugs and gangs, and was working as a pizza delivery driver to pay for community college classes. In the boy's eyes, James was a hero—an example of the best that life could offer. When the teacher asked what the boy wanted to be when he grew up, his answer was simple: "I want to be just like James."

The boy's vision of success was limited to what he saw as the most extraordinary option in his world.

We Can Only Aspire to What We Can See

From the time we're born, our environment is the lens through which we understand what is possible—and what isn't. The stories we hear, the examples set for us, and the things that are emphasized (or discouraged) become part of our *programming*, silently dictating the boundaries of what we believe is achievable.

In my own family, it was clear that going to college was non-negotiable. Both of my parents had made the choice to pursue higher education, despite coming from backgrounds where college wasn't expected. My mother, in particular, had to fight against her father's wishes, secretly applying to college and then announcing she needed a ride to campus with her bags already packed.

Growing up, I absorbed this message: **College was just something you did**. It wasn't until high school when I encountered friends whose families held different, loftier expectations, that I realized not everyone grew up with the same assumptions. For some of my wealthier peers, it wasn't just about going to college—it was about getting into *the best* colleges, preferably Ivy League universities.

The differences between my family's expectations and my friends' were stark, but they also taught me something crucial: when the bar is raised, so is the scope of what you believe is possible.

Possible vs. Impossible

Our environment, while shaping our view of the world, plays a huge role in whether we believe something is possible or impossible. For example, we in the Western world (especially those of us with any amount of privilege) often take for granted things like iPhones, reliable transportation, and access to clean water. But for millions of people around the globe, these aren't guaranteed. And the divide doesn't stop there—it extends into the realm of opportunity and career possibilities.

What may seem *impossible* to one person may feel like a perfectly reasonable aspiration to another.

In some families, becoming a US senator, an Emmy award–winning actor, or a Harvard Law professor feels within reach. In others, it feels like an absurd fantasy.

In the United States, we ask students to declare a career path at eighteen when choosing a college major. In the UK, it happens even earlier—at fifteen or sixteen. But think back to yourself at fifteen: how many career options were you aware of? Probably just what you saw on TV, what your parents did, and the careers of the people immediately around you—whoever showed up to Career Day in your third-grade class. How likely were you to dream about becoming a virtual reality designer or a podcast producer when those careers didn't even exist yet?

This shows just how critical *exposure* is. Here's a list of ten careers that didn't exist twenty years ago:

~ AI Engineer
~ Driverless Car Engineer
~ Data Scientist
~ Cloud Architect
~ Social Media Manager
~ Podcast Producer
~ Digital Strategist

~ Sustainability Manager
~ Fintech Analyst
~ App Developer

And in the arts, new possibilities continue to open up:

~ Virtual Reality (VR) Experience Designer
~ Twitch Streaming Artist
~ 3D Printing Artist
~ Digital Costume Designer for Virtual Avatars

The landscape of what is possible is constantly evolving.

Programming from External Influences

Our family, friends, and society at large play significant roles in determining what we perceive as possible. These messages, which often go unquestioned, can plant deep roots in our psyche. Perhaps your family viewed creative careers like acting or music as irresponsible, or even ridiculous. Certainly, those were not "real jobs." Over time, those voices may have shaped your beliefs about what was or wasn't a valid career option.

On the flip side, you may have grown up in a family like mine, where pursuing a Liberal Arts degree or going to a music conservatory was seen as not only viable, but noble. The quiet, unspoken messaging in my household told me that it was the people "just out to make a lot of money" who were the problem. The artists would save humanity.

For me, the world of classical music felt like home. From a young age, I was surrounded by elite musicians—people in the Chicago Symphony Orchestra, world-renowned string quartets, and esteemed pedagogues. To my teenage self, it was not only possible to become a professional cellist; it was the **only thing I knew to do**. In hindsight, I realize that wasn't true, but the belief had been programmed into me so strongly that I never even considered other paths. This is common to all families. Everyone is raised from a different but distinct set of thoughts, rules, and assumptions. There are certainly many people who will live their entire lives according to those thoughts, rules, and assumptions—passing them along to their own children without ever questioning them, but I think it's helpful—healthy even—to pop open the hood and poke around a bit. Let's do that now.

Exercise: Exploring the Roots of Your Programming

Take a moment to reflect on your upbringing and the messages you received about careers and possibilities. Use the following questions to guide your thoughts:

1. What careers did the people closest to you have when you were growing up?

2. What kinds of things were considered possible in your household?

3. Were there any careers, lifestyles, or dreams that seemed impossible or even discouraged?

4. What external influences have shaped your current career and life choices?

Such reflections will help you uncover patterns in your programming that may be influencing your present decisions. I will help you figure out what to do with this new information in Parts II and III of this book. For now, your only job is to notice what's there.

The No-Yes Spectrum: Turning "No, Because" into "Yes, If"

Many of us are familiar with the voice inside our heads that says, *No! You can't do that*, any time we even think about doing something new. Whether it's career related, like going back to school later in life, or auditioning for that community theater; or life related, like signing up for a marathon, or moving to a new city, or getting bangs. A small, almond-shaped part of your brain called the amygdala, or what psychologists call the "**lizard brain**," is responsible for our fight, flight, or freeze responses that hit us in those moments. Over time, we develop habits of saying, *No, because...* to almost everything new or risky simply to keep that lizard brain quiet:

~ Can I become a doctor? "No, because medical school is too expensive."

~ Can I move to France? "No, because I don't have an EU passport."

~ Can I make millions of dollars? "No, because I'm terrible with money."

Sound familiar?

Now imagine what happens when you switch to a *Yes, if ...* mentality. Here's how it works:

~ Can I become a doctor? "Yes, if I create a plan to cover the costs of medical school and seek scholarships."

~ Can I move to France? "Yes, if I look into visa options or work-abroad opportunities."

~ Can I make millions of dollars? "Yes, if I gain some financial literacy and create work that serves people with what they want and need."

This shift opens up new possibilities, allowing you to move from a place of limitation to one of creativity and opportunity. Instead of being stuck in a *No, because ...* mindset, you're actively exploring what *could* work. *Yes, if...* gives you power.

Right now we're just exploring what other possibilities might be available to us with this slight reframing. There's no need to make any big decisions just yet. (Often, this exercise will have people wanting to move to France, *and* go to medical school, *and* train to be an astronaut!) Just open up those possibilities, and we'll sort the rest out in Part II.

Exercise: Turning No into Yes

Look at an area of your life where you feel stuck—where you've been saying *No, because ...* for too long. Maybe it's a career change, a creative pursuit, or a move to a new city. Write down your own *No, because ...* reasons. Then challenge each one by flipping it into a *Yes, if ...* statement.

Example: Can I go back to school and get another degree?

- *No, because I don't have enough time to take classes.*

- *Yes, if I rearrange my schedule and take one class at a time, I can gradually earn the credits I need.*

Challenging Your Assumptions

Ultimately, re-assessing your inner programming means taking a hard look at the assumptions you've been carrying around—about yourself, your potential, and what's possible for your future. These beliefs are often invisible, yet they control your choices and limit your growth. In this first chapter, you have considered how your upbringing, your environment, and your own protective brain have left you with a set of ideas around what was or was not possible for you. Who you are now, what you do for your career, and how you move through life is, in large part, due to that inner programming you've been carrying around. By completing the exercises throughout this chapter, we have taken aim at those beliefs—questioning and challenging them in order to gain a clearer understanding of who we are, and how we got here.

Here's one last one to tie it all together:

Exercise: The Possibility Journal

On one page, list five things you were programmed to believe about what you couldn't (or weren't allowed to) do. Then, on the other side of the page, rewrite each belief, turning it from *impossible* to *possible*.

Write about why you had that limiting belief in the first place. Was it a scared parent trying to keep you from getting hurt or rejected? Was it because of your environment? Was it because you remember your favorite uncle talking at the Thanksgiving table one year about how people with money were jerks, and it's stayed with your forever?

Do a little daydreaming. For each belief, write about what your life would be like if you were living out the possibility. What would life be like as an astronaut?

By identifying and rewriting these internal narratives that have been limiting you all these years, you can begin to understand and break free from the programming of your past. It's your first step in creating a more expansive and intentional future.

2

Re-Assessing
Your Old Stories

To be yourself in a world that is constantly trying to make you something else is the greatest accomplishment.

— Ralph Waldo Emerson

Stories About Your Circumstances

When re-assessing our current situation, it's essential to closely examine what's working for us, what isn't, and why. As we saw in the last chapter, sometimes the trajectory of our lives is laid out by others, but it all might not be so terrible! There are, I'm sure, aspects of your life that you absolutely love and would never trade. In my case, while it's true that music, and the cello in particular, was chosen for me when I was young, as an adult it became my responsibility to decide if that narrative still served me.

I remember my first meeting with Lisa, who was a burnt-out wreck at the time she booked her first call with me. I knew her as a music colleague. She and I had played some chamber music together years before and she was a great player. Since then, she had devoted her career to music education, working a full-time position at a Title I public school while also maintaining a robust private studio. Music education wasn't just a passion for Lisa—it was her whole identity. But between her 7:30 a.m. to 3:00 p.m. school job and her private teaching sessions most afternoons and evenings, she was barely functioning, let alone thriving.

She often spoke with deep conviction about the importance of public school music education and her commitment to giving children of all backgrounds access to the arts. Yet, in nearly the same breath, she would tell me how exhausted she was, how she often resented the challenges and long hours of the job—and that she dreamed of leaving.

Lisa was conflicted. She had internalized a narrative that told her that in order to be a good person, she had to serve others at the expense of her own needs and desires. But the disconnect between her values and her daily life was simply becoming unbearable.

She was also trapped by another deeply ingrained story: the belief that one must choose between teaching music and playing music, but doing both was not an option where she lived.

"It's just the way things are here," she'd tell me over and over again.

The reality, though, was that she desperately missed performing. She longed to get back to the stage and participate in the "real gigs" in her area, but she felt paralyzed by the stories she'd told herself about what was possible.

I'm happy to report that, with time and a great deal of reflection, Lisa found a way to break free from both her job and the old stories that were holding her back. After re-assessing her life and letting go of her old narratives—that is, allowing herself to turn what was previously deemed *impossible* into *possibly possible*, she handed over her public school position to someone equally passionate about music education and instead focused on her private studio and performing career. She also took on a leadership role with a global organization that provides music lessons to economically challenged children, allowing her to channel her passion in an even bigger, more balanced way.

According to a recent Gallup poll, 67 percent of US workers feel disconnected or dissatisfied with their careers, often staying due to financial security, fear, or lack of perceived alternatives. Lisa's story mirrors this statistic, but her eventual success shows that, with courage and clarity, we can rewrite our own stories.

These old stories that we're carrying around with us can appear as beliefs or habits. Really, beliefs are nothing more than thoughts we've rehearsed enough times to make them feel like truth. Lisa's old narratives were based on habitualized beliefs:

1. Good people sacrifice themselves for the greater good.
2. Musicians must either teach or perform. You can't do both well.

We all do this in one way or another. As we discovered in chapter 1, our parents, caregivers, or cultural surroundings instilled ways of being that we adopted as truth. For example, in one household, it may be customary to have a cocktail after work, while in another, alcohol may be forbidden altogether. Each family assumes the other is doing it wrong because they're living according to different narratives.

When I was growing up, my family ate dinner together every night. It was non-negotiable. But my best friend's family had a different story—her family grabbed meals on the go between their chaotic schedules of baseball, football, choir rehearsals, and more. They thought we were strange for having a daily sit-down meal, and I thought they were just as strange for not doing it.

Stories About Your Habits

Those inherited narratives—the inner programming we received from our family—can turn into our daily habits as we become adults and begin living our own lives. Without thinking about why, you might find yourself on autopilot, insisting on sitting down for dinner, or always grabbing dinner on the go. *Always* having a drink after work, or *never* having a drink after work.

How many of the habits and beliefs you carry today are inherited, either consciously or unconsciously? Do they still serve you? Or are you, quite literally, living out old stories that have long since expired?

Exercise: Re-Examine Your Daily Habits

Take a moment to walk through your typical day. Identify your habits and see if you can uncover the underlying stories behind them. For example:

- **Morning Routine:** *I wake up at six every morning* (HABIT) *because early risers are successful. Only lazy people sleep in!* (STORY)

- **Coffee Ritual:** *I always grab a large coffee* (HABIT) *because I need it to survive the day.* (STORY)

- **Teaching Schedule:** *I teach all day on Saturdays and Sundays* (HABIT) *because that is the only time students are available to have lessons.* (STORY)

Once you identify these habits and their associated stories, ask yourself whether they still serve you. Do you even still believe the stories to be true? Or have the stories become as habitualized as the actions themselves?

I used to tell myself I needed a lot of coffee to get through the day. This stemmed from years of working eighteen-hour days, seven days a week—from a 5:00 a.m. practice session to classes, rehearsals, and afternoon teaching, which melted into evening concerts and a long commute home. I never had enough sleep, never had enough time, and I was exhausted all the time. Coffee was what kept me upright and alert—both behind the wheel and behind my cello.

But today? I get my eight hours of sleep, and while I still love a good cup of coffee, I no longer rely on it to fuel my entire day. The story that *I need a lot of coffee* no longer holds water.

These old stories affect everything about our lives. Has the story *TRUE artists don't do it for the money* led to you to stay in financial stress out of the fear that making money might mean you're not a *TRUE* artist? Or has the story *Only people from certain crowds win Grammys* kept you from recording the album at all? Identifying and re-assessing such stories gets us another step closer to high-fiving our ideal self.

I should note that not all stories are inherited. Some we adopt willingly. As I mentioned at the top of this chapter, at fifteen, I made the *conscious* decision to pursue a career as a professional cellist. There was nothing I wanted more. But by the time I turned forty, my priorities shifted. The old story that *classical music is the only thing that matters* simply didn't resonate with me anymore. It had served me well before, but holding onto it in midlife felt *off*, and was causing me more anxiety than fulfillment.

Exercise: Re-Assess Your Old Priorities

Write down five things that were once crucial to you, but are no longer as important—or perhaps not important at all. This could be anything from drinking Diet Coke, to spending time with a certain person, to being an actor. Just write down the first five things that come to mind.

1. _____

2. _____

3. _____

4. _____

5. _____

Now, dig deeper. What are the old stories you're currently wrestling with? What parts of your life no longer fit, even if you're reluctant to let them go? (For example: *No longer crucial—Maybe my friend Jill? We were always so inseparable—hitting the bars, laughing, singing, we always had the best time, and I felt so cool when I was around her. But now we've grown up a bit, life has taken us in opposite directions and we just don't have that much in common. Hanging out feels awkward and forced, and I just feel depressed and down after seeing her.*)

1. _____

2. _____

3. _____

4. _____

5. _____

Habits Are Only Good If They're Intentional

Habits can be powerful tools for success, but only if they align with who we are and where we want to go. James Clear, in his book *Atomic Habits*, emphasizes the importance of intentionality in habit formation: "Every action you take is a vote for the type of person you wish to become." If we are not intentional, our habits can keep us stuck in old patterns, preventing us from moving forward.

We'll dive deeper into habit formation in Part III of this book, but for now, it's essential to look at your current habits and distinguish between *Current You* and *Past You* behaviors.

Exercise: Categorize Your Habits

Look through your daily routines and habits, and sort them into two categories: Current You and Past You. Find at least five habits from your past that no longer serve you. You might want to pick a few from the earlier exercise in this chapter.

1. _____

2. _____

3. _____

4. _____

5. _____

When I've done this exercise with clients, they're often shocked by the results. One client realized she was still saying "no" to weekend plans "in case she got a gig," even though she now had much more control over her schedule. Another was still smoking because he had adopted it as part of his "cool artist" persona in his twenties, but quitting became easy once he reframed his identity.

How many did you find that are no longer serving you? How can you pivot that habit or that time into something useful for current you? What is something that would feel more aligned with who you currently are? If you want to give up your habit of drinking Diet Coke throughout the day, can you swap it out for a flavored seltzer water or green tea? If you want to give up your habit of saying "no" to plans, you can instead form a habit of making weekend plans each week if you haven't been offered a gig by Wednesday.

Exercise: New Habits

1. _____

2. _____

3. _____

4. _____

5. _____

Stories About Your Future

The stories we tell ourselves about our future can be just as limiting as those about our past. In chapter 1, we explored how the options presented to us as children shaped who we became as adults. But now that you're here, as a fully functional adult, what possibilities do you see around you?

Future-based stories often begin with phrases like "I could never ..." or "I'll never be...." These kinds of beliefs set invisible boundaries around your potential.

There's a difference between stories that relate to your current circumstances and those that relate to your future. Stories about your circumstances sound like, "I can't because ..." while future stories sound like, "I'll never ... or I could never...."

For example:

~ *I can't run because I'm too out of shape.* (current circumstance)
~ *I could never run a marathon.* (future story)

We'll tackle the former first, then break down the latter. Often, these stories we've held onto about our current circumstances are the ones keeping us tethered to outdated narratives and determining the thoughts we have about our future. It ties back to what we think is *possible* versus *impossible*.

There are several excellent coaching exercises that can help you reframe a story you've been telling yourself that is keeping you stuck.

Two of my favorites are The Model, a classic exercise named here by Brooke Castillo, founder of The Life Coach School, and The Work, by Byron Katie. Both are excellent resources and I highly recommend them both. What they have in common is a method to question your thoughts around the story you've been telling yourself about your circumstance.

Recall my client Lisa; she was telling herself two unhelpful stories about her circumstance: 1) if she stopped teaching in the public schools it would mean she didn't care about music education; and 2) where she lived meant she had to choose to either teach or perform—she wasn't *allowed* to do both.

Reframing those stories involved breaking those statements apart and asking deeper questions:

~ What *other* reasons could one have for leaving a full-time teaching position?

~ What *else* might "Caring about music education" look like?

~ *How* might teaching *and* performing help a person become better at both?

~ *Who* decided it wasn't allowed?

~ What *was* she allowed to do in her career? And *who* does she need to run her ideas by, exactly?

Often these stories we've been believing and living our lives in accordance with, sound downright ridiculous when we take a step back, break them down, and question them. But that's what we're here to do, right? Re-assess what we've been blindly accepting and agreeing to? In doing this exercise, you might decide that you still wholeheartedly agree with some of your stories. That's wonderful! No one is suggesting your life is 100 percent terrible. We're after the other ones, though. The stories that not only aren't serving you, but could be doing harm to your chances of becoming that ideal *beyond potential* version of yourself.

Exercise: Your Three Stories

Try to lock in on three stories you have about your circumstances, and write them out here:

1. _____

2. _____

3. _____

And now break them apart into smaller pieces, and dig deeper into each part, as we did above.

1. _____

_____

_____

2. _____

_____

_____

3. _____

_____

How were you able to reframe things? The circumstances probably didn't change, but your stories about them probably did. What conclusions did you draw?

The Accidental Story or, My Retirement Party

Before moving to Bermuda, I had what many would call a dream career as a freelance cellist in Boston. It's one of the world's greatest cities for classical music, and I played in some of the best groups, taught at prestigious festivals, had a private studio filled with amazingly talented students, ran the chamber music program for one of the largest youth orchestra programs in the world, and held a nearly full-time contract as the Director of Orchestras and Chamber Music at an elite school. By most people's standards, I had made it.

I was so busy that I didn't realize how deeply unfulfilled I was. One day, a non-musician colleague mentioned my future retirement party. She imagined my former students forming a little orchestra, playing Grammy award–winning recordings that I had been a part of, and as she continued to detail this imagined future, I broke out in a cold sweat.

This was not the legacy I wanted to leave behind. I didn't want to be remembered as the high school orchestra conductor or for a series of recordings I was hired to perform on just because I happened to be in the right place at the right time.

It was at that moment when I realized I had been drifting off course for years. If I wanted my life and career to reflect my values and passions, I had to change course myself. No one was going to hand me a better narrative. I had to write my own.

How aligned is your present with how you see your future? Are you where you need to be in order to get there? It's possible that you're here reading this book because you're not sure where you see your future. Maybe you were striving toward one end, and have decided that's not for you. Maybe you're here just feeling a bit lost. That's okay—I've got you.

But if you are quite clear on what you want the end of your career to look like—if you can see every minute of that video montage showing on-screen as you're being giving that lifetime achievement award, but you're currently doing something completely different? It's time to re-assess.

If you want to be known for your contributions as a producer, for instance, but you're still taking bit roles in community theater, we need to re-assess. If you want to be celebrated for your innovations in the world of content creation, but you're doing the same old, same old week after week, it's time to re-assess.

Stories About Your Future

Let's go back to those future-based stories: *I'll never be able to quit teaching, I could never make a living as a performer, It's too late for me to switch careers, I'm too old to learn how to play the guitar,* and so on.

There are hundreds of variations of these statements, but they all serve the same purpose: to box you in. Most of these stories are grounded in fear or insecurity, but mixed with the inner programming, and long-held limiting beliefs. They feel like the undeniable truth because they've been repeated in our minds over and over.

A well-known psychological phenomenon called the self-fulfilling prophecy suggests that if we believe something to be true, we act in ways that make it true. If you tell yourself, "I'll never be able to make a living as a performer," you will likely stop looking for performance opportunities, neglect your practice, and avoid networking with other performers. In doing so, you practically ensure that the future you imagine becomes reality. It's the classic story of the kid who's told they're not good at math, believes it, and never tries to improve, thus becoming exactly what they feared—a bad math student.

But what if you could *interrupt* those stories? What if, instead of thinking, "I'll never be able to make a living as a performer," you started thinking, "What would it take for me to make a living as a performer?"

Here, we're going to use our new *Yes, if ...* thinking strategy on our locked-in limiting beliefs. This single shift in mindset can open up a whole new world of possibilities for you.

The Power of Rewriting Your Future

In the book *Mindset: The New Psychology of Success*, psychologist Carol Dweck discusses the concept of a fixed mindset versus a growth mindset. People with a fixed mindset believe their abilities are set in stone; they're either born talented or not, smart or not, capable or not. Those with a growth mindset, on the other hand, believe that abilities can be developed through effort, learning, and persistence.

When it comes to your future, adopting a growth mindset is the key to rewriting your story. Instead of limiting yourself with thoughts like "I'm too old or I'm not talented enough," you can shift your perspective and ask, "How can I grow into the person I want to become?"

Let's take the example of Sophie, another of my coaching clients. Sophie had been a dancer her whole life, but at the age of thirty-eight, she started feeling like her best years were behind her. She loved dance, but she had this nagging belief that she was "too old" to continue a performing career and should settle into teaching full time. But when I asked her what she *really* wanted, her face lit up.

"I want to keep dancing," she said. "I just feel like I'm supposed to stop. I feel like no one will take me seriously as a dancer anymore because I'm older."

Together, we worked on dismantling that story. What were the facts? Was it true that no one would take her seriously because of her age, or was that just a story she had told herself based on societal norms?

As it turns out, it was the latter. From that starting point, we discussed what it would take to get Sophie to where she wanted to be. She began to seek out performance opportunities that were age-inclusive, and she also recommitted herself to getting back into peak-performance shape. She auditioned for roles that suited her experience and maturity rather than competing for the younger, stereotypical ingenue roles. She also started choreographing, a skill she had long wanted to develop, but had convinced herself she wasn't ready for. Sophie is now performing regularly, and her choreography has been featured in several productions.

Her transformation came from one simple shift: questioning the old story she was telling herself about what was possible.

The Stories Society Tells Us

As creatives, we're often bombarded by societal expectations that shape the stories we tell about ourselves. Whether it's the myth of the starving artist or the idea that it's too late to change careers after forty, we're constantly influenced by external narratives that may not serve us.

For example, society often paints the picture of success as linear—where you set a goal in your twenties, work tirelessly to achieve it, and then spend the rest of your life reaping the rewards. But for most of us, success doesn't look like a straight line shooting upward and to the right. We grow, change, and evolve, and the paths we once thought were perfect for us may no longer fit as we learn more about ourselves and the world around us.

This is particularly true for creative careers. Artists, musicians, writers, and performers are expected to follow a certain trajectory: train in your craft, reach the peak of your field, and then either teach or retire quietly. But these narratives don't allow for the natural ebbs and flows of a creative life. They don't account for periods of reinvention, exploration, or personal growth.

Let's face it. Societal stories can be stifling, especially when they are built on outdated notions of success, fulfillment, and age.

My own experience as a cellist was fairly linear in the beginning. I had great first teachers, practiced, won some competitions, lost more, went to prestigious summer festivals, and then a prestigious music school, had the validation of receiving scholarships for all of it, won a spot in the New World Symphony—the preeminent training ground for future orchestral musicians—Spoleto, USA, and spent my summers at Tanglewood in western Massachusetts. My career was headed in a clear 45-degree angle, up and to the right.

But then I took some detours. Instead of doing what I was *supposed* to do, and win a big job straight out of New World, I decided to stop taking auditions and move back to Boston. There were further detours into the Dahlia Piano Trio and other explorations into chamber music—which turned into running various chamber music programs for talented students. Further detours took me into the world of contemporary music—which is what all of the best players did (society told me so!)—except I didn't really enjoy playing it as much as I enjoyed the friends I had there. Regardless, by the time I hit my early thirties, my razor-straight line toward success had formed a few curves. It continues to this day as well, but if I zoom out, the curves lose their power and the line appears to straighten again, continuing upward and to the right.

And whether it's because of indecision, or because you felt compelled to follow your curiosity, or because you took time off to raise a family, travel around the world, care for your aging parents, or whatever it was you did, your nonlinear career path only means one thing.

You're doing it right.

Breaking Free from Societal Expectations

One of the biggest hurdles creatives face is the pressure to conform to societal standards, whether in terms of financial success, career paths, or the definition of *artistic value*. How many of us have internalized the story that being an artist means struggling financially, or that pursuing something outside of our art somehow makes us less of a creative?

I once worked with a visual artist named Ben, who had spent years grinding away at his studio practice. He was talented and had achieved moderate success, but he felt like he was spinning his wheels. He wanted to explore other avenues, such as opening a gallery or launching a collaborative arts space, but he held back because he feared that stepping outside of the pure artist role would make him a sellout.

"Where did that idea come from?" I asked him one day. "Who told you that being an artist means you can only focus on making art, and nothing else?"

Ben realized that his idea of what it meant to be a *real* artist had been shaped by teachers, peers, and even the media he consumed. He had internalized a narrative that equated artistic purity with creative success, even if that success meant barely scraping by financially.

When he finally broke free from that story, Ben went on to open a successful gallery that became a hub for local artists and art lovers alike. He still makes art, but he no longer feels confined by the old narrative that was limiting his definition of success, and keeping him stuck.

I can't tell you how many times my own career decisions have butted up against societal stories that I had been told my whole life.

1. "Orchestral freelancers can't be soloists" ran through my brain as I started booking my first solo recital tour.

2. "You have to live in a major city if you want to be a successful musician" crossed my mind as I packed up my condo in Boston and moved to the tiny island of Bermuda.

3. "People only trust big-name conservatories to create new programs" seeped into my thoughts as I launched what would later be seen as a groundbreaking online international summer festival during the 2020 COVID pandemic lockdown.

The above statements weren't just my own amygdala's protective thoughts. These were actual phrases that colleagues and friends said to me at the time. They meant no harm, and those words were said out of love, care, and respect for me, but I hoped they were wrong.

Guess what? They were.

Exercise: Rewrite Your Future Story

Take a few minutes to reflect on the stories you've been telling yourself about your future. What assumptions are you making about what's possible? What fears are holding you back? Write down your current future story in as much detail as possible.

_____

_____

_____

_____

_____

_____

Now, write down what thoughts, ideas, beliefs, and advice you're ready to let go of. Even if you aren't sure what you might do without these beliefs.

1. _____

2. _____

3. _____

4. _____

Moving Forward

As we wrap up this chapter, it's important to remember that the stories we tell ourselves shape our reality. Whether they're stories about our past, our habits, our circumstances, or our future, these narratives influence the choices we make and the paths we take.

By identifying the old stories that no longer serve you and rewriting them in a way that aligns with your true values and desires, you are creating space for growth, possibility, and fulfillment.

In the next chapter, we'll explore what happens when we realize that our stories and habits have taken us way off course.

3

Re-Assessing Your Path: What to Do When Your Career Has Taken a Wrong Turn

The best time to plant a tree was twenty years ago. The second-best time is now.

— Chinese Proverb

If Not Here, Then Where?

Animal trackers will tell you that getting off the track is always a part of the process. It's important to know where the animal *hasn't* been so that you can narrow its location down. And the same is true for tracking our own paths through life. As Martha Beck discusses in her book, *The Way of Integrity*, finding yourself in the "Path of Not Here" can be seen as a fortuitous moment.

"Right! Got it! Time to Turn Around and Head Somewhere Else."

There are several scenarios that would lead a person to discover they weren't where they needed to be on the path of life. For some people, the destination was known all along, and they might have even set off with a good map of the best possible path. Slowly but surely over the years, however, they somehow inched themselves off course— much like me and my retirement party story. Others charge down the road that they *think* is the right path. They power forward with vim and vigor, quite sure that this is the way, only to reach the end of it and realize their car is not in this parking lot after all. They've spent months, years likely, heading full-force in the wrong direction.

And, of course, sometimes people have dutifully marched down the right path toward the right destination, only to be confronted by a bear, or a landslide, or an injury that prevents them from continuing on. They're on the right path, but they are most definitely not where they need to be or even want to be. Take for example, the principal dancer faced with a chronic foot injury, or the Broadway actress taking in a devastating diagnosis just as whispers abound that she's a shoo-in for a Tony. Sick kids, sick parents, an unexpected divorce—there are a hundred different ways for life to disrupt you.

And, of course, you might have picked up this book because, while on the surface everything looks perfectly peachy, you know, deep down, that you have found yourself on the wrong path, heading toward a destination that you're less than excited about.

We're going to get you back on track.

Now what?

For a person in this situation, realizing they are *not* where they want to be, and looking at dozens of different trail signs all veering in different directions, things can feel daunting. So daunting, in fact, that they might choose to just hang out on the (wrong) trail for a while and make themself at home.

I can see it in the eyes of a new client when I ask them what they want their career (or life) to look like and they look downward and sheepishly say, "That's the problem. I don't know. I just know that this isn't it."

One of my clients, Adam, was in that same position. Having quit the corporate world, he knew he wanted to be an artist. He just didn't know what *kind* of artist. A sculptor? A painter? Mixed-media? Photography? He was paralyzed by indecision, feeling that he had wasted too many precious years already and didn't have time to experiment. He wanted to figure out what he wanted, and then just go for it. Pedal to the metal.

But it doesn't always work that way.

What DO You Know?

I asked Adam to get quiet for a second. To sit still and just listen. And then I asked him this question: "What DO you know?"

"No, I *really* don't know anything," he pleaded. "I want you to tell me what I should do."

"Just tell me one tiny thing you know you want in your life," I responded.

And after a minute, he said this: "I know that I want to wake up every day knowing that I am going to be making some art."

And so we started there. For the next thirty days, he didn't need to find any more answers. His only mission was to wake up every day and at some point in the day, make some art. Any kind of art. From there, clarity started to form—albeit very slowly. He started enrolling in a few art classes, figuring out what he was good at, what excited him, what he was naturally drawn to. He realized he had been asking himself the wrong question. It wasn't that he needed to figure out what medium to work on, he needed clarity around what he wanted to say with his art. Who was Adam as an artist? The question he really needed answers about was, "What was my art about?" not "What is my art made of?"

As those answers crystalized for him, he entered a local competition—the theme of which aligned beautifully with his artistic mission. Then he started posting his work online and showing it to others, and is currently working on his first solo show. He's been able to see more of the path he wants to be on, and it came out of asking, one step at a time, *What DO I know?*

Often, those little truths that we know, deep down, are difficult to admit to, because they are in cognitive dissonance with those old stories we spent chapter 2 dismantling, and sometimes they are difficult to latch onto because they seem so insignificant. I promise you; they are not. Here are some examples of small clues that we can latch onto:

- ~ The globe-trotting soloist who knows he wants to be home for his child's birthday
- ~ The freelancer who knows they want to perform outside of their own city
- ~ The accountant who knows she wants to grow roses in her yard
- ~ The cinematographer who knows he is fascinated by chefs and the art of food creation
- ~ The dancer who knows she is also interested in climate justice

So, What Now?

If you thought being lost was scary, just wait. Because identifying the *right* path—the one that is perfectly aligned with your soul and your values, the one you know in your heart is *your* path—can seem like a terrifying and daunting task.

You can see it, right there, but there are a lot of uphill bits, and there's a waterfall you're going to have to get around (don't worry–it's stunning!) and what's worse, you now can't *not* head out on this path.

Also, you're too old to be starting over, aren't you? It's quite possible you're not experienced enough. Or maybe you're too young, or too fat, too skinny, too wealthy, too poor, too … pick your excuse.

Now, tie up those laces. We're heading off.

We all know the famous story about the painter, Grandma Moses, and how she didn't become a professional artist until she was seventy-eight years old. As an avid artist as a child, she set her creative pursuits aside to make way for more practical activities like farming—until, that is, she had enough, and set out on her path to become an artist in her later years.

Or Colonel Sanders, who didn't get into the food industry until he was in his forties and didn't start his fried chicken empire until he was sixty-two years old! I'd say that worked out well for him.

Any time someone utters the phrase, "Well, it's too late now." "That ship sailed a long time ago." Or "You can't teach an old dog new tricks," or some such quip, they are forced to come to terms with this evidence that anyone can change their life trajectory at any time.

My student Isobel's father was a prominent and highly respected physician. But he had originally trained as a jazz bass player. It wasn't until after having his second child that he decided to go to medical school—in his forties—(gasp!). He finally became a practicing physician in his early fifties and ended up becoming a leader in his field at a major hospital in Boston.

Okay, okay, I see you nodding in annoyance. I get it. Some people manage to make midlife career shifts. But how?

Don't worry. I've got six entire chapters dedicated to everything you need to know about the *how*. But before we get there, we have to determine the *what*.

Exercise: Journaling

Zoom out for a bit on yourself. Where are you? Where are you headed? Which path(s) did you take? What's around you?

Write that down here:

_____

_____

_____

_____

Now, list all of the things that you enjoy about where you are. Your teaching position? Your students? The creative work you get to do? Your schedule? Where you live? Your partner? Your dog?

1. _____

2. _____

3. _____

4. _____

5. _____

And then list anything that isn't working for you right now. Your teaching position? Your students? The kinds of opportunities you've been offered lately? Your schedule? Where you live? Your partner? Your dog?

1. _____

2. _____

3. _____

4. _____

5. _____

Addressing What's Not Working

Before we dive in to Part II and start figuring out what your amazing new life is going to entail, let's address the things in your life that aren't working for you. From the list above, choose three things that aren't quite working for you right now. Now, no BS—what would it take to either eliminate it or fix it? Narrow it down to five important steps.

Say, for example, you were unhappy in your faculty teaching position because the schedule was awful, the commute was dreadful, and the pay is worse. No BS. What would it take to fix it or eliminate it?

1. *Look into whether you could teach during a different day/ time, when traffic isn't so bad.*

2. *Compile a list of your contributions to the school, such as positive reviews from students and colleagues.*

3. *Revise your resume, LinkedIn profile, and personal website.*

4. *Schedule a meeting with your superior to discuss schedule changes, and renegotiate your pay.*

5. *Apply to other school positions.*

And if you wanted to lose some weight and get healthier, for example, your five steps might look like this:

1. *See your doctor to get blood work done and discuss.*

2. *Hire a nutritionist.*

3. *Hire a chef or meal service to provide healthy meals.*

4. *Hire a personal trainer who can help you stay consistent and avoid injury.*

5. *Clear your house of tempting treats.*

Or let's say you want to run a marathon:

1. *Buy some good running shoes.*

2. *Join a running group.*

3. *Carve out time each morning and on the weekends to train.*

4. *Hire a trainer.*

5. *Sign up for incrementally more challenging races throughout the year, like a 5K, 10K, half marathon, and finally, the marathon itself.*

For most people, getting themselves to take these actions is hard enough (that's what Part III of this book is for) but while we're reassessing our inner programming, old stories, and where we are right now, it can be helpful to see that it *is* possible to get yourself unstuck. Whatever is not working in your life or career right now, there is a way to fix it or eliminate it. In doing so, you'll be making room for all of those wonderful things your ideal self is itching to do.

4

Re-Assessing
Your Associations
(A Brief Word About
Your Friends and Family)

You are the average of the five people you associate with the most.

– Jim Rohn

This is a controversial quote by the godfather of personal and professional development, Jim Rohn. It always conjures up protestations like, "That would be my family! That doesn't make sense!" Or, "Are you saying I should give up on my oldest and dearest friends because they aren't successful enough?" Well, no, of course not. But it is true—especially in the arts—that the people you associate with the most are the people you're going to be most like.

Exercise: Your Inner Circle

Excluding your immediate family members, write down the five people you tend to hang out with, talk to, or work with the most:

1. _____

2. _____

3. _____

4. _____

5. _____

Next, write down five traits and values you would like to see in your life (for example, fit, intellectually curious, kind, funny, financially comfortable):

1. _____

2. _____

3. _____

4. _____

5. _____

Now go back to your list of five people. For each one, give a tick for each of those five traits they embody. What do you notice? Are you pretty aligned with your top five? Or are you struggling to get up for your 6:00 a.m. runs because your friends want to stay out for a long night of "beer, burgers, and bangers"? If you're feeling good about the level of alignment, that's great! It's the ideal. You probably find that you unofficially keep each other accountable and on track. Keep nurturing those traits in yourself and in them, and continue being each other's biggest supporters.

Not so aligned? You're not alone. And no, I'm not going to tell you to ditch your oldest and dearest friends. At the end of the day, no matter what, we all have more in common than not. I'm assuming you are still friends with these people because you love them, share a long history, and they have enough material to blackmail you for decades.

Expanding Your Network

I am, however, going to urge you to find some other people to surround yourself with—even if the friendships aren't as deep. Even if they're temporary. These new associations don't need to threaten your closest inner circle, but you're missing out by not finding people who are more aligned with where you are and what you want to do.

For example, if you want to get in shape, you could start hanging out with people who are heading to the gym regularly (or the yoga studio, or the running trails—whatever your thing is). If you want to land your first Broadway show, then you can find some like-minded people who will go to tap class with you, listen to your monologues, and share studio space with you. Want to develop your leadership skills? Interact more with people who are starting or heading up organizations, who can share ideas about board development or setting up an LLC or a 501(c)(3).

One of my favorite aspects of Creatives Leadership Academy, my group program for creatives, is the effect that being surrounded by other creatives who are in similar stages of life and career development has on the participants. Being in a room full of smart, awesome humans, all of whom are interested in creating bigger, bolder lives for themselves and their families makes their dreams feel perfectly normal—sometimes for the first time ever.

When you look at that list of five traits and values that you'd like to see in your life, whose faces come to mind? Who do you know who embodies those traits, or is also striving for them? Are there colleagues at work who are doing the kinds of things you'd like to be doing? Make an effort to get to know them. Here are a few other ideas of where to find these new friends:

- ~ An investing club
- ~ A neighborhood book club
- ~ A cycling or running group
- ~ An audition prep program
- ~ A group coaching cohort
- ~ A writing group
- ~ An adventure group
- ~ A gardening co-op
- ~ A wine circle

Your new friends and associates might not ever reach "chosen family" status, but that's okay. They will still teach you a lot about what you are capable of, about what is possible in the face of what you previously believed to be impossible. It's all relative, after all.

I remember the first time I went to lunch at my friend Amy's house. Amy had moved to Bermuda to start her own reinsurance company. That, in and of itself, is pretty impressive. We met at a Bermuda Philharmonic Chamber Music event I was hosting and it was there that I learned of her love of classical music and the arts, in general. I received an invitation soon after to a luncheon she was hosting at her home for a few "badass ladies" she had met since moving to the island. I only recognized one other name—my friend Sylvia, another reinsurance CEO, who also plays violin in the Philharmonic. Definitely a badass.

Around me at that lunch table were eight incredible women— business owners, C-suite executives, and nonprofit leaders. I found myself surrounded by female leaders, all of us engaged in a completely different level of conversation. Where my kindhearted freelancer friends were discussing how to send postcards to help elect their favored candidate, these women were talking about hosting large-scale events and raising millions of dollars for a campaign. And while grassroots work is important, being a part of a conversation that bats around numbers in the millions and billions like it's nothing certainly inspires you to start playing a bit bigger.

Remember, it's all relative. Get yourself around people who make your wildest dreams seem like a walk in the park.

5

Re-Assessing Your Dreams: Meeting Your Potential Self

Someone once told me the definition of hell: The last day you have on Earth, the person you became will meet the person you could have become.

– Anonymous

A Paradigm Shift

Now that you have an understanding about the programming you inherited and have a better understanding of your own self-imposed limitations, I want to flip the script. What if, instead of being governed by your limiting beliefs and old stories, you were guided by a sense of innate possibility?

The opening quote tells of a hellish scenario, in which, at the very moment it's too late to do anything about it, and those limitations are suddenly revealed to you. You are faced with the version of you who lived free of such limitations, who instead lived with the belief that you could do anything—that whatever you truly desired in life was possible. This version of you stands before you, almost mocking your life.

Sounds dreadful.

But since we're here talking about it, we have the opportunity to loosen its grip on us. The idea of this ideal version of us is no longer a sudden realization, but information that we can use to guide us in the right direction.

If Step One was to dig deep to see our inner programming, limiting beliefs, and worn-out stories for what they are and start looking beyond them, then Step Two is to reach out and grab the future we want.

I talk a lot about the idea of potential. As artists, it seems our lifelong pursuit is in reaching it, sometimes losing ourselves (and often our friends and family) in the process. My work as a coach is about helping people and organizations reach their own true potential, rather than the potential that was dictated to them at a young age, or by society itself. That work is about defining it, getting past the mindset obstacles in the way of them reaching it, or figuring out how to both reach that potential *and* have a normal, healthy life with all that such a phrase means to you.

Is it possible to achieve your potential if you're not dedicating every waking moment to your craft? I believe the answer to that question depends on how you define *Your Potential*. It's easy to take what you do—such as a cellist, basketball player, singer, dancer, poet, etc.—and compare it to whomever is considered the Best of the Best in that field (for example, Yo-Yo Ma, Michael Jordan, Maria Callas, Martha Graham, Maya Angelou).

Growing up, wanting nothing more than to have a career as a cellist, I would see the glamorous soloists, hear the stories passed down, and experience my own stories of intermingling with these stars. To my fifteen-year-old self, it made sense that to meet my potential as a cellist meant to be the best cellist in the entire world.

But that's only one area of my life. At fifteen, it was the only one that mattered—save whomever my latest crush was—but at fifteen, we're not always aware of what life is really all about.

What happens when we grow up and we want to reach our potential in our career, but also in our role as spouse or parent, or even reach our potential financially? What if you have additional new pursuits that appear, and then you want to reach your potential as a painter, or an interior designer, or a gardener? If becoming the Best of the Best requires 100 percent focus, then by definition, we can't be the best of the best at more than one thing.

But what if we re-defined our potential to reflect our own personal best? What does that look like? How do we find it? And how do we pursue it?

I once heard a story mentioned on a podcast, almost as a side-note—though it's safe to say it was one of those moments that changed everything for me—about a man who died and instead of being greeted by Saint Peter at the pearly gates, he was greet-ed by the version of himself that had fulfilled all of his truest, most hidden dreams. This entire book is centered around that question: "What if, when you die, you go to heaven and you're met by the version of you who reached their potential—their *real* potential?"

Doesn't that just stop you in your tracks? I found it both terrifying and fascinating. What would Kate-who-met-her-most-true-and-real-potential even be like?

What was fascinating to me was what that "ideal" Kate *hadn't* done. She wasn't a Superstar Best of the Best Cellist of All the Land—and in an instant, I realized that it simply wasn't that important to me anymore. She had lost those extra pounds I'd carried around since I was in middle school, and her teeth were straight (wait, I was supposed to *wear* that retainer? Oops!). In meeting her, I knew very clearly what her house looked like, what her social life was like, and that she was a writer.

That was the moment I realized that I had always secretly wanted to be a writer, but I had chosen cellist, so ... oh well. It never occurred to me that both of those pursuits could find space in my life. Thankfully, she was still happily married to my husband Paul (phew!), so I knew I had gotten at least some of it right.

From the macro to the micro, what became clear to me was both what I would regret *not* doing, and what *wouldn't matter* to me in the slightest. If I met that Kate and she was a brain surgeon, I'd probably think, "Oh, that's nice for you," but I didn't miss not being a brain surgeon in my version. I would, however, look at her perfectly straight teeth and kick myself. *Man, all it would've taken was a few months of Invisalign!*

Vulnerability and the Honest Truth

The hardest part of this exercise for most people is confronting those things about themselves that they hide from everyone else—their discomfort with their relationships, or their body, or the fact that they have talked for years about learning French and still couldn't even order a croissant on the Champs-Élysées.

Beyond the small details like straight teeth or that stubborn ten pounds, there are, of course, the big things too. The realization that you're in the wrong career, or that you don't have the kind of life you want, or the fact that you know, deep down, that you are capable of so much more than you're doing, capable of doing the things you *want* to be doing, capable of earning the income that would allow you to sleep better at night, capable of performing at the level you want to be performing, capable of starting that scholarship fund for students.

Capable of doing the things that you keep, for some reason, putting off.

And it requires us to get honest with ourselves. What *are* those things? And why are you not doing them?

Having it All

What happens when your *Potential Self* is both a world-class … something, and also a fully present family man? How does that work? Can you do both? Can you do it all? If the example is George Clooney—movie star, and father to seven-year old twins—then yes, but it takes a lot of money, a team of nannies, and a house on Lake Como. But for us mere world-class mortals, I think the answer lies more in the idea of being both things at various times—fully on tour, and then fully present at home.

My childhood friend Kirsten was the daughter of a cellist—a very well-known one—who was on tour for much of the year. But they were an amazing family, and he was an amazing dad. I remember him being both super involved in her life, and also often away performing. Both could work. Both could be true.

Exercise: True Desires

If time, energy, and money weren't obstacles, and I could do everything I wanted in life (and do them well) I would:

1. _____
2. _____
3. _____
4. _____
5. _____
6. _____
7. _____
8. _____
9. _____
10._____

Regrets

"But what about regrets?" My friend Tivin asked over one of those fancy hotel buffet breakfasts. We were discussing this idea of meeting your potential self, and that was where her mind went first. "What if this potential version of me didn't make any of the mistakes I've made? Or, What if they did do things I regret not doing in my past? I mean, there's no going back—so I've already messed it up, right?" Hmmm. Very good questions. The only thing I was regretting in the moment was not having gone to the omelet station, but I understood what she meant.

I regret not keeping in touch with some of my mentors—most of whom are no longer alive. I regret not taking harder classes in high school. I, like all classical musicians, regret not practicing more when I was eight. And I regret not wearing my retainer when I was in middle school.

But that's the whole point. Confronting ourselves with our potential self *now* allows us to see which regrets will really and truly bother us at the end of our lives, and maybe the whole point of this exercise is to make amends while we can. Do I regret that I didn't take harder classes in high school? Or do I regret that I never learned calculus? Because while I can't go back to my junior year, I *can* learn calculus if I want to. Especially since I live with someone who teaches calculus.

Do you regret not keeping in touch with a specific person? Or do you want to be the kind of person who stays in touch more now? If it's the latter, who can you reach out to today?

Exercise: Mitigating Regrets

In the left column below, make a list of things that you regret—either things you did that you regret doing, or things you didn't do that you regret. On the right, list how you could mitigate or remedy that regret now. For example, "I regret not taking harder classes in high school; I can learn calculus and Latin now."

Regrets	*How to Mitigate*

I believe we should strive to reach our fullest potential, but I also believe that we need to get honest and quiet, and we have to take the time to define that potential for ourselves. My fullest potential will look completely different from yours. What truths lie beyond our original version of potential are unique to each of us. That's what makes them so wonderful. And what makes the idea of missing out on them so heartbreaking.

The Best vs. Your Best

Remember that your *Potential Self* is unlike anyone else's. There's no one right and true version of potential. The idea of "the best" that you've been living with was very likely handed down from someone else. In any given industry, the idea of what constitutes this is purely subjective. "The best" for one lawyer could be sitting on the Supreme

Court. For another it's being head partner at the top law firm in New York. For another, it's trying war criminals at The Hague, and for another, it's representing underserved communities or the environment in ways that make a big difference.

When I talk about *THE* best vs. *YOUR* best I'm not implying that there's "the best" and then there's the lesser level you are capable of achieving. I simply mean, what is *your* version of "the best"? What does that mean to you? What would you be so wildly excited about achieving in your career, in your life?

I'm not looking to be a world champion bodybuilder; I'm just looking to feel comfortable in my own skin. For me, that would be the best.

Maybe your version of "the best" isn't the same as your family's or colleagues' versions. That doesn't matter. What matters is that, at the end of the day, you're leaning into *your* version.

Ask Yourself, "And Then What?"

Sometimes it's hard to judge where we want to be on the spectrum of "the best." What, exactly *do* we want? And how much of it? I want to be a writer, but do I want to be a Michael Crighton or James Patterson type of writer who churns out a book or two every year? Hmmm. Here's a scenario that will help you figure it out, at least for now.

Let's say you know that your Beyond Potential Self loves to grow her own food, but … to what extent?

Does she have a vegetable garden?

"Yes."

And then what?

"And she built a greenhouse or polytunnel set up to extend the season with indoor growing."

And then what?

"And she got some backyard chickens so she could have fresh eggs."

And then what?

"And then she bought some land and started a farm...."

And suddenly you stop yourself.

"No ... that's too much! I don't want to be tied to a farm year-round. That's a ton of work that I'm not interested in. Just the veggie garden, the greenhouse, and the chickens."

If you push it even a little too far, you'll know. Find that sweet spot that sounds almost too good to be true, but you'd be so psyched if it happened. Some examples could be:

> ~ The point where you're in demand as a performer, but not to the point where you haven't seen your kids in three months.
>
> ~ The point where you have the pick of the litter when it comes to the students you're teaching, but before the point where you're teaching seven days a week between three different schools.
>
> ~ The point where you have a seat at the table, but before you're the one in charge.

Or maybe you *are* the one in charge. It's up to you.

We all want something different, and that's the whole point.

Assess the Required Steps

For each scenario you described above, think about what it would be like to head in that direction, and list the steps that would be required to accomplish it. Use the "No BS, what would it take?" method we talked about in chapter 3. Whether those steps are in your control or not. For example, fix crooked tooth (make an appointment with the dentist, and come up with a plan); get a tenured professorship (work on résumé, create and publish a legacy piece that is written or performed, apply for jobs and get some interview coaching, network with colleagues, etc.). Whatever the goal is, no matter how out of reach it seems right now, you must see it as a done deal—that version of you did it, therefore, you can too—and have a list of action steps you can take to get yourself there.

Exercise: Journaling

Take yourself to that moment of meeting the version of yourself who did all the things you want to do. Describe that person in detail. What do they look like? What have they done? What do they do? What does their house look like? Their car? What do they do in their spare time? Get it all down on paper. Write until you can't think of anything else to write about. Write about their relationships, their work, their proudest accomplishments. Write about the clothes they're wearing, the car they are driving, and the people they spend their time with. Look at their bank accounts—how are they doing financially? What are they doing with their money? Also pay attention to how they seem. Calm? Happy? Energetic? Warm? Cool?

In describing them, keep checking in with that sense of personal alignment. Are you assigning them awards and accolades because they represent success in your field? Or because you truly desire that recognition? Both options are valid, but only one is true (for you).

What surprises you about them? Are there things that come up that you had kept buried deep inside for years? Things you had even forgotten you care about? Or were there things that you thought you'd care more about, and just … don't? Or is there, like is the case with most of us, a combination of both?

In Part II, we'll be taking the information you've gained about this version of yourself and using it to re-define who you are, where you're headed, and how you interact in the world. Free of all of those limiting beliefs, old stories, and concern over where you are on your path, you'll be able to spell out a future (and a present) that is more fully aligned with who you really are.

TWO

Re-Define

Clarifying the Vision: What Lies Beyond Your Potential

6

Re-Defining Your Life's Compass

If you can dream it, you can do it.

— Walt Disney

In Part I, we discovered more about who you are and how you became that version of yourself. In Part II, we'll be taking that already-awesome you and re-defining what you are capable of; what your *true* dreams are. We're going to be re-defining how you want to be seen, what you want your legacy to be, how you see yourself, how you explain yourself to others, and generally speaking, how you move around the Earth.

And we'll set some goals in place that will help you get there.

For some of you, this might turn out to be a huge glow-up, where you end up virtually unrecognizable from your previous "self." For others, it's more of a subtle tweak—an expanded set of possibilities here, a greater understanding of your roles and behaviors there. But for anyone working through this book, this middle section will leave you with the kind of clarity around you, your work, your purpose, and your capabilities that you have only dreamed of. And with this clarity, you'll be free to start living your life in a way that leads you to becoming your Beyond Potential Self.

Beginning With the End in Mind

Have you ever written a eulogy? Talk about a high-pressure gig: you have to somehow summarize a person's entire life in ten to fifteen minutes, including their accomplishments, their passions, values, and loves. You have to convey what this one, unique person was all about, how they were different than all of the other one, unique persons out there in the world. Oh, and don't forget to be heartfelt and serious, and make sure there are some funny bits thrown in, as well, to bring a few moments of levity.

This time, the assignment is a little bit easier … or harder, depending on how you look at it. After all, there's no one in the world you know better than yourself. We're starting with a nod to Stephen Covey who, in his book *The 7 Habits of Highly Effective People*, famously introduced this exercise in his similarly named chapter. The idea of writing one's eulogy has roots in philosophical and coaching traditions that encourage contemplating one's legacy as a way to live with greater intention. Additionally, research in psychology has shown that reflecting on one's mortality can help foster a deeper sense of purpose, leading to a more authentic and fulfilling life.

Morbid? A little, but there's no better exercise in discovering what is truly important to you than to determine what you want people to say about you when you're gone (and what you definitely do *not* want them to say about you). The exercise of writing your own eulogy is a powerful tool for reflection and invites you to pause and think deeply about the impact you want to make By imagining what others might say about you at the end of your life, you can clarify your core values, reveal the qualities you hope to embody, and uncover the goals that matter most to you. The practice is often used in personal development and coaching as a way to help individuals align their daily actions with their true aspirations— which is exactly what we are here to do.

Exercise: Writing Your Eulogy

When you think about your legacy, what are three things you want to be remembered for?

1. _____
2. _____
3. _____

How would you like family, friends, and colleagues to describe their relationships with you? What role did you play in their lives?

1. _____
2. _____
3. _____
4. _____
5. _____

What accomplishments, both personal and professional, would make you most proud to have mentioned in your eulogy?

1. _____
2. _____
3. _____

Which core values guided you throughout your life? How did you embody these values in your daily actions?

1. _____
2. _____
3. _____

How did you impact the lives of those around you? Who would say you made a difference in their life, and how?

1. _____
2. _____
3. _____

If your life had a theme, what would it be? What overarching purpose or passion did you pursue?

What lessons or insights do you hope others learn from your life? What wisdom do you want to pass along?

1. _____
2. _____
3. _____

What challenges or setbacks did you face, and how did you overcome them? How did these shape your character during your life?

1. _____
2. _____
3. _____

What are the moments or experiences that define your life? What do you want people to remember you by?

1. _____
2. _____
3. _____

Exercise: Journaling

Write out your eulogy in full, and include all the information you mentioned above. What themes come up for you? What do you notice?

Exercise: Questions to Consider

If today were truly the end, what would you regret not having done? What goals, dreams, or relationships need more of your attention?

Re-Defining Your Call to Work

Do you know what your life's purpose is? I'm not sure I do; and if I'm being honest, I don't know too many people who can say (with absolute certainty) what their life's purpose is, either. It can feel like a lot of pressure to figure out our true purpose, and I'm not entirely sure we can know that answer ahead of time—it's one of those determinations that's usually made in hindsight. However, we *can* point ourselves in a direction that feels true to us, something in alignment with our values and skills.

When I first started doing this work in earnest, my clients were primarily classical musicians. It was the spring of 2020, and most of them had just seen all of their work get canceled for the foreseeable future due to the COVID-19 pandemic. Figuring out ways to make money to buy groceries and keep the lights on was paramount, and while some of our colleagues went out to get real estate licenses or learn computer coding, most wanted to be doing work that they enjoyed and that felt like they were using the skills they already had. I would go through this exercise of skill-stacking (figuring out one's unique combination of skills, experiences, and passions) with them, and it created some enormously creative (and successful) side hustles like musician-specific fitness and nutrition consulting; an online music and movement summit; videos of one-act operas; short two-, three-, and five-day summer intensives for students; and more. Others would go on to create ongoing programs and events that are still making an impact (and generating an income) years later!

This skill-stacking process is a series of four different exercises created to help you home in on your natural gifts and inclinations. We'll be looking at these questions through different lenses. We will consider how you like to work, the kind of work that feels most like you, the intersection of your skills and preferences, and the needs of the wider world, and then try to condense it all into one concise sentence. Here we go.

Exercise: Your Core, Intuitive Role

All humans have a core, intuitive role, and if we can keep that role at the forefront of whatever job we are doing, we will find joy and fulfillment. Consider which of the following you are:

A. Teacher: You're always the one who volunteers to show the new person around. You love sharing ideas, knowledge, and skills about everything from the perfect way to boil an egg to passing down your craft to the next generation.

B. Creator: You're happiest when you're making something come alive—especially if it has never before existed. You're the composer, the painter, the chef, the photographer, or the choreographer of your life. Give yourself a blank canvas or a block of free time, and you will bring the magic.

C. Curator: You could spend hours putting together the perfect concert program, art exhibit, menu, or speaker lineup for a summit. You love playing around with different combinations and you geek out over clever, hidden connections.

D.   Investigator: Do you have a PhD? Do you want one? You love to dive deep and get every bit of knowledge you can about something. You love researching program notes and historical backgrounds. You will spend hours researching the best vacuum cleaner on the market. You're on never-ending search for the truth in all things.

Answer: At heart, I am a _____.

Exercise: Your Favorite Moments

For this exercise, I want you to go back to your childhood memories and think of a time between the ages of one and eighteen when you were doing something that required skill-based work (for example, anything from baking cookies with Grandma to mowing the neighbors' lawns, to acting in your high school play). The key is that this was a moment when you felt completely alive and connected with your truest self—a time when you felt completely and genuinely *you*.

Memory: _____

What was it about this moment that's compelling for you? For example, was it the connection you felt to your grandmother? Or the sense of independence you felt when she let you measure the ingredients all by yourself? Did you love the feeling of trust and responsibility from your neighbors, or was it the first time you realized you could earn money from an idea? Was it being in the spotlight in your play, or was it the sense of being a part of a team?

The key feeling: _____

Can you boil that feeling down to one word (for example, "community," "team," "connection," "responsibility," "independence," etc.)?

My one word: _____

Do this exercise two more times. The second time should be a moment from young adulthood, and the third time should have taken place in recent years. Recall doing some kind of "work" where you felt the most like yourself. Figure out what it was about that moment that made it so special, and then narrow it down to a single word.

My second word: _____

My third word: _____

You might have landed on three different words, or you might have landed on one common one. There's no right answer, but you can add those three words to your list of clues about the kind of work you could be doing to bring you the most satisfaction.

It doesn't necessarily mean that you need to change jobs, but you might see a key piece that has been lacking. Maybe one of your words was "spotlight." But you're a devoted teacher who spends their time helping students achieve the spotlight instead. How might you get yourself into the spotlight once in a while? Have a cameo in the school play? Perform a piece in your studio recital each semester? Join a local improv group?

Ikigai

The concept of *ikigai* is a Japanese philosophy that represents "a reason for being," or the intersection of purpose and passion that makes life meaningful. *Ikigai* is often thought of as the balance of four elements: 1) what you love, 2) what you are good at, 3) what is needed and 4) what you can be paid for. By achieving harmony between these aspects, a person can find a deep sense of purpose and joy in daily life.

Historically, the concept of *ikigai* has been associated with longevity and well-being, particularly among the people of Okinawa, a Japanese island known for its high proportion of centenarians. Okinawans don't typically retire in the Western sense. Instead, they continue to engage in the work they love throughout their lives, which they believe contributes to their health and happiness.

The following Venn diagram illustrates the intersection of the four elements mentioned:

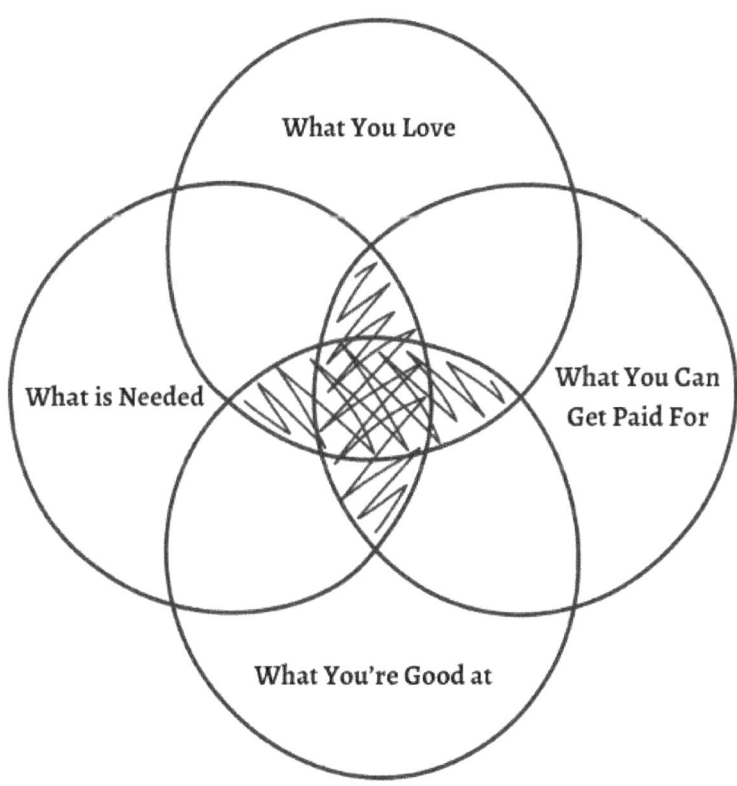

To answer the first part, *what you love*, you can pull in the three words you came up with in the previous exercise. You might love cinematography, but now you've identified that you feel most alive when you're working as part of a team. So, "I love cinematography" becomes "I love cinematography and being part of a team."

Exercise: Five Things I Love

1. _____
2. _____
3. _____
4. _____
5. _____

Exercise: Five Things I'm Good At

To find your answer(s) to this second part, you can add in your core, intuitive role (for example, music, personal development, writing, speaking, coaching, teaching).

Five things I am good at:

1. _____
2. _____
3. _____
4. _____
5. _____

Exercise: Five Things the World Needs That I Could Provide

To answer this part, again, lean into your core, intuitive role. If you're an Investigator at heart, how could the world benefit from a deeper understanding of your beloved topics? What does the world need to learn from the Teachers among us? What connections and relationships could the Curator help the world to see differently? And what could a Creator make that would make the world a better place?

If the "world" is too intimidating, let's take it down a notch and see if the answer lies in your own community. The world might not need another orchestra conductor, but Bermuda did when I stepped in as music director of the Philharmonic there. It's a role that brought together my favorite skills of coaching, encouraging, music (and time management!), and allowed the Teacher in me to thrive.

Five things the world (or community) needs that I could provide:

1. _____

2. _____

3. _____

4. _____

5. _____

Exercise: Five People or Organizations That Would Pay

The next part is about money. We can't all work for free all the time, and the idea of the starving artist has run its course and died a slow death. We're done with that old trope. Let's make an income, shall we?

Five people or organizations that would pay for the kind of work identified in the previous exercise:

1. _____
2. _____
3. _____
4. _____
5. _____

The One-Sentence Challenge

See if you can name the following famous people from these descriptions:

1. A theoretical physicist best known for his theory of relativity, which revolutionized our understanding of space, time, and gravity

2. A pioneering scientist who won Nobel Prizes in both physics and chemistry for her groundbreaking research on radioactivity

3. An Indian leader who used nonviolent civil disobedience to lead India to independence from British rule

4. A trailblazing media mogul, philanthropist, and talk show host who rose from poverty to become one of the world's most influential women, using her platform to inspire, empower, and give back

5. A Renaissance polymath, whose works in art, science, and engineering, such as the *Mona Lisa* and *The Last Supper*, have left an indelible mark on culture and knowledge

6.   A Mexican painter known for her self-portraits exploring themes of identity, suffering, and resilience

7.   An English playwright and poet whose works, such as *Hamlet* and *Romeo and Juliet*, are some of the most influential in the English language

Answers: 1) Albert Einstein; 2) Marie Curie; 3) Mahatma Ghandi; 4) Oprah Winfrey; 5) Leonardo da Vinci; 6) Frida Kahlo; 7) William Shakespeare

Did you get them all? You likely got most of them right off the bat. Each of these great men and women is well-known for their accomplishments, but they achieved those accomplishments because of the *clarity* of their vision and work.

Remember that re-defining your goals is not about abandoning everything you've worked for, or even drastically changing who you are. Instead, it's about expanding your understanding of yourself, clarifying your values, and ensuring that each step forward aligns with your deeper intentions.

Through the exercises in this chapter, you've been challenged to think about your legacy, identify your core values, and reconnect with what brings you joy and fulfillment. This clarity provides you with the freedom to move confidently toward a life that feels truly meaningful. Embrace this opportunity to refine your direction and take purposeful action toward your Beyond Potential Self. Each small decision you make from here on out is another brick laid in the foundation of the life you're building—a life designed by *you*, with intention, depth, and authenticity.

Exercise: Descriptions

To end this chapter, I'm challenging you to write a pair of one-sentence descriptions of yourself. The first is a description of who and where you are right now. Maybe the sentence is: "Right now I'm a bored, out-of-work actor trying his best to figure out how to live a happier and more purposeful life." Whatever your sentence is, make sure each word is true for you right now.

Right now, I'm _____

_____

_____.

And then for the second sentence, write the description based on the person you wrote your eulogy for in the first part of the chapter. Write the version of you who had achieved your wildest dreams, made a difference in the world, lived with purpose and passion, and then add your name. For example, "Oscar- and Tony award–winning star of stage and screen, who spearheaded a national initiative to support and mentor child actors and brought about necessary changes to the industry." (your name)

_____

_____

_____.

7

Re-Defining
Your Identity

Life isn't about finding yourself. Life is about creating yourself.

– George Bernard Shaw

In chapter 6, we zoomed way out in order to get a better idea of the direction you want to take—particularly with the kind of work you want to be doing. We took a hard look at the big-picture issues like your values, skill sets, sense of purpose, the overall themes that bring you the greatest sense of joy and fulfillment, as well as how you want to be remembered. We also looked at the kinds of accomplishments, relationships, and legacy you want to be known for after you're gone.

In this chapter, let's zoom back in to your inner being. Imagine yourself standing in the middle of an empty room—a single human being made up of a body, a mind, and emotions. All three parts need to be addressed with intention in order to bring the current version of you up to the standard of the Beyond Potential version of you, and that's exactly what we'll be doing now: comparing one with the other, and figuring out which gaps need to be filled.

Re-Defining Your Physical Identity

There's a growing trend that revolves around "body hacking" and physical optimization, with scientists like Andrew Huberman and physicians like David Attila giving us insight into ways to optimize our bodies, our sleep, our minds, our longevity. Follow their advice, and you, too, can become the perfect physical specimen and live to be 150! And while the focus of this book is becoming the best version of yourself, the key (as you discovered in Part I) is that you are embarking on becoming *your* ideal version of yourself—not anyone else's ideal version of you. Not even the ideals of famous scientists and physicians.

Maybe your ideal version *is* completely optimized. Maybe you yearn to develop the discipline required to never touch a drop of caffeine or alcohol again, and to do anything and everything you can think of to live as long as possible.

That's great!

Or, you might have found, back in chapter 5, that your *Beyond Potential* version of yourself preferred intense belly laughs with friends over sit-ups as your chosen abdominal workout. Perhaps your ideal way to honor your physical body is to have time each morning to do some gentle yoga and eat a delicious breakfast of eggs and bacon, and even a soft, buttery croissant—carbs be damned!

No one is here to judge your ideal, Beyond Potential Self. But you should have as much clarity around what you want your body to be able to do, feel, and appear as you do around your work goals. You only get one body, and it's up to you to take care of it—whatever that means to you.

Exercise: Fill in the Blanks

Take a moment to check back in with your Beyond Potential Self (the one you met in chapter 5) and then complete the following statements:

My Beyond Potential Self's body is different from mine in that _____.

My Beyond Potential Self's favorite form of exercise is _____.

Something physical my Beyond Potential Self can do that I can't do yet is _____.

My Beyond Potential Self gets _____ hours of sleep each night.

One physical thing I admire about my Beyond Potential Self is _____.

If I were to describe my Beyond Potential Self 's physical appearance in three words, they would be _____, _____, and _____.

If I were to describe my current physical appearance in three words, they would be_____, _____, and _____.

A few physical traits I already have in common with my Beyond Potential Self are_____, _____, and _____.

Exercise: Goal Setting for Your Physical Self

What are three goals you would like to set for the next year to get yourself closer to your Beyond Potential Self physically?

1. _____

2. _____

3. _____

Building Your Ideal Intellectual Self

Imagine your mind as both a library and a workshop—a place where knowledge, skills, and creativity all come together to build and refine the person you want to be. The purpose of this section is to help you reconnect with your current mental strengths and potential, clearing away any clutter that's keeping you from achieving clarity and growth.

We'll be exploring the skills, knowledge, and intellectual habits that define you right now—and those you need in order to build a richer, more fulfilled life. This is not about aiming for a one-size-fits-all, *smarter* version of yourself; it's about finding out what skills and knowledge resonate with your Beyond Potential Self's interests and aspirations, and making a plan to actively cultivate them. Let's begin to create a blueprint for your intellectual growth, one that aligns with the goals, dreams, and vision of your ideal self.

Let's start with today's version of you. What are your current areas of intellectual strength? I have a musician colleague, Steve, who can tell you the key of every major symphony in the orchestral repertoire. I have another friend, Kris, who has an encyclopedic knowledge of movies (especially *terrible* movies). Much of this, of course, has to do with a person's educational background and career. A musician is more likely to have a vast amount of knowledge around symphonic literature than an accountant.

Take stock, for a moment, of what your areas of strength are, and where you might be a bit weaker in areas that you would like to be more knowledgeable or proficient in. I don't know a damn thing about car engines, but I also don't feel like I'm missing out. I don't have the periodic table of elements memorized, but I don't really need to, except when it comes up occasionally as a pub quiz question. Besides, my husband (a science teacher) does, and he's on my quiz team, so I'm good. I *do*, however, wish I knew more about ancient history. I don't know why, but I do. My Beyond Potential Self is quite knowledgeable about history from the time of Mesopotamia to yesterday's news, and she can carry on intelligent conversations and connect more dots due to her knowledge of this history. I was feeling a bit jealous.

In her 2006 book, *Mindset*, psychologist Carol Dweck asserted that people exist on a spectrum of belief around where ability stems from. On one side of the spectrum is what she calls a "fixed mindset," where people either have an ability or they do not. For instance, a child is either born with artistic talent or they will remain doomed to a life of drawing stick figures. On the other side is the belief in a "growth mindset," the idea that anything can be improved—performance, knowledge, or skill—"with effort, good teaching, and persistence."[1]

Obviously, having more of a growth mindset is the more optimistic, more productive choice, and more conducive to tightening any gaps you see between your current knowledge base and that of your Beyond Potential Self. The knowledge that no matter what it is you want to learn, you can do it, allows us not only to see possibilities for future selves, but to be motivated to go after them. Recall my former student's father—the jazz bass player who went to medical school in his forties. There was definitely a growth mindset at play there. Understanding that with some effort, good guidance, and a bit of

---

1 James Morehead, "Stanford University's Carol Dweck on the Growth Mindset and Education," OneDublin.com, June 19, 2012, https://onedublin.org/2012/06/19/stanford-universitys-carol dweck-on-the-growth-mindset-and-education.

persistence, there is nothing you can't learn, I've been studying my ancient history almost daily, and loving every minute of it.

Assuming that anything is possible, what would you learn?

Exercise: Setting Intellectual Goals

What are three goals you would like to set for the next year to get yourself closer to your Beyond Potential Self in an intellectual sense?

1. _____

2. _____

3. _____

Strengthening Your Emotional Self

The third aspect of our identity that we're going to look at here is our *emotional* side. Emotions are powerful guides—they shape our decisions, influence our relationships, and color our experiences of the world. It's crucial to have a clear understanding of how these inner forces are affecting us, and learn to navigate and even harness them, rather than letting them control us.

In this section, we'll explore how you process emotions, respond to stress, and relate to others, with the goal of helping you build a stronger, more balanced emotional foundation. Developing emotional resilience isn't about suppressing difficult feelings or always being positive; it's about cultivating the self-awareness and skills you need in order to handle life's highs and lows with grace, balance, and authenticity. As we dive in, let's consider the kind of emotional life you might want to create for yourself—one rooted in self-compassion, clarity, and a genuine connection to those around you.

In my coaching practice, I work with the belief that the client has the answers they are seeking within them already, and it's my job to help them come to those answers through asking questions. It's *not* my job (nor is it helpful to them in the long run) to give advice or tell them what *I* think they should do. Occasionally, though, it can be helpful to hold up a gentle and compassionate mirror to certain default behaviors they have. It could be a tendency to blame others for their misfortune, or to play the victim in every situation. I had a client who used to take everything personally. If a student was in a bad mood during their lesson—clearly, it was her fault. If her teenage son made a snide remark to her, clearly, it was because she was a terrible mother. It never seemed to occur to her that the student could be feeling guilty and embarrassed because they didn't practice all week, or maybe they had a bad day at school. Or, maybe my client's son was just being a typical teenager, experimenting with pushing buttons and boundaries.

Other clients would default to different behaviors, such as:

~ Creating drama
~ Resisting ideas (their own and others)
~ Criticizing
~ Judging
~ Taking actions based on false assumptions
~ Making excuses

Those examples all came from high-achieving adults who otherwise had successful lives and careers, but these default emotional reactions were getting in the way of moving forward. It can be challenging to bring about a strong awareness to our own tendencies. As the saying goes, "It's hard to see the label from inside the bottle," but it behooves us to try. Of course, we're all human, and we all have our off moments, but if we consistently default to less-than-helpful behavior, it's better to identify it sooner than later so that we can figure out a solution. If you want, you can enlist a trusted partner or close friend to help you.

Let's do a quick check-in on some of the more common emotional defaults that can get in our way.

Exercise: Common Emotional Defaults

Put a check in the column that most reflects you.

How often do you:	Often	Sometimes	Rarely
Criticize another person			
Blame someone else			
Resist help from others			
Think someone is mad at you			
Put aside your own needs for another's			
Focus on the worst-case scenario			
Insist on your own perfection			
Bury your emotions			
React defensively to criticism			
Lose your temper			

When it comes to managing those moments better, several strategies can help you pause and give yourself a beat. Here are a few:

~ Deep Breathing: Taking three to five deep breaths gives you time to center yourself before reacting.

~ 3-2-1 Technique: A classic mindfulness trick: Identify three things you can see, two things you can hear, and one thing you can smell in the moment.

~ Somatic Check-In: Ask yourself what you're feeling, and where you're feeling it (for example, "My face feels hot," or "I feel like there's a heavy boulder in my stomach").

With time and practice, you can identify your default behaviors, learn to recognize when you're exhibiting that behavior in the moment, use one of these methods to catch yourself, press pause, and then redirect your behavior, thought, or response.

I've found it helpful to find a simple question I can ask myself, such as:

~ "Could it be something other than me that is causing them to behave this way?"
~ "What if she is really doing the best she can?"
~ "How might their criticism be a helpful guide for me?"

When you consider your Beyond Potential Self, and how they move about in the world emotionally, what differences do you see between them and your current self? Are you in awe of their ability to stay calm under pressure when you often lose your temper and start shouting? Do you wish you could be less of a perfectionist (or more of a perfectionist!) like them? Do they have an ability to connect with others that you would love to develop?

Exercise: Your Beyond Potential Self's Emotional Strengths

My Beyond Potential Self exhibits more emotional strength

by _____, and

_____, and they

also _____. And

they never seem to _____.

Exercise: Emotional Strength Goals

What are three goals you would like to set for the next year to get yourself closer to your Beyond Potential Self in terms of emotional strength?

1. _____

2. _____

3. _____

Re-Defining Your Taste

While we're here taking a deep dive into your identity, we might as well talk about your likes and dislikes. This section might not be about *re*-defining anything. What I have found in working with clients, is that we often have no idea what our tastes are. Can you tell me your favorite color? Favorite dish? Favorite ice cream flavor? I bet you could when you were five, but as we grow into adulthood a favorite color can turn into "whichever color shirt is clean and ironed this morning." Our favorite dish has become "the one I didn't have to cook." And a favorite ice cream flavor can be "whichever flavor my kids like because that's what we end up buying anyway."

I was working with a client who was getting ready to attend a big event where she would be a featured guest. I asked her to describe this future event in the most ideal light. She went about describing the venue, the other people there, that the green room wasn't too cold (now that *is* ideal!), and she lit up as she spoke about what she was wearing—a beautiful, cherry red jumpsuit. She was so excited about this jumpsuit that I assumed it was waiting in her closet at home. "Is that your favorite thing to wear?" I asked.

"Oh, I don't own it—it's just what I would want to wear," she said.

It wasn't the fact that it was a jumpsuit that was ideal, it was the color. "Red makes me feel powerful," she said. "And I just really love that color."

If your next thought is, "I bet she doesn't actually own anything in that color," you'd be right. She loved it, but had forgotten that she loved it. It came out that her favorite dress as a little girl was red—her grandmother had made it for her. And red and white were the colors of her beloved elementary school, but she hadn't owned anything red in years. "It's funny," she remarked, "I don't think I even have anything red in my house, but I really do love it."

Sometimes it's the connotations of something that keep us from having it around. You might know that you love flowers, but you associate having fresh flowers in your house with a certain income bracket. When you're wealthy, *then* you'll have fresh flowers in your house.

In reality, you could pick up a decent bunch of flowers at the grocery store for less than you spend on lunch. What a small price to pay for something that brings you so much joy! There's no need to wait until some future moment.

Checking back in for a moment with your Beyond Potential Self, what are the things that they like? How can you start to incorporate more of those things into your current life?

Exercise: Your Beyond Potential Self's Likes

Complete the following statements through the lens of your Beyond Potential Self:

1. A color they love to wear is:

   _____

2. Their clothing style could be described as:

   _____

3. Their favorite thing to eat for breakfast is:

   _____

4. Their favorite go-to restaurant is:

   _____

5. They never leave the house without:

   _____

6. Their favorite holiday is:

   _____

7. Their favorite ice cream flavor is:

   _____

8. Their dream vacation spot is:

   _____

9. Something they like to collect is:

   _____

10. Their favorite kind of music is:

   _____

As we wrap up this chapter, take a moment to recognize the depth of the work you've done here. Re-defining your identity across the physical, mental, and emotional realms isn't just about adopting new goals or mindsets; it's about honoring the person you want to become by actively shaping each part of yourself with intention and clarity. Remember, the journey toward your Beyond Potential Self is less about *fixing* anything, and more about aligning your actions, choices, and beliefs with the person you've always known you could be.

Every step you take, every insight you gain, is a piece of the mosaic that forms a life of purpose and fulfillment. Embrace the possibilities ahead with the confidence that this self-reflective work is the foundation for everything you're meant to build. You are, quite simply, creating yourself.

8

Re-Defining Yourself
to Others

*You have to be brave with your life so that others can be brave
with theirs.*

— Katherine Center

Are you feeling like a new person yet? It's one thing to re-define
our lives to ourselves. Even just that work can feel intense and
exhausting. In Part I, you went through your entire childhood, family
stories, habits, behaviors, and picked apart every step you have taken
in life to determine whether it was a step you wanted to take, or a
step that was dictated to you. Then, in the last two chapters, you have
re-defined or recommitted to your purpose, your values, and your
entire identity. It wouldn't be unusual if you suddenly find yourself
walking differently, seeing things differently, acting a little differently,
dressing a little differently (you picked up that red sweater you saw at
the store the other day, didn't you?).

Other common symptoms at this point in the process are:

~ A greater ability to self-regulate in tense situations
~ A clearer understanding of the skills and talent you bring to the table
~ Strong desire to learn Portuguese or Italian
~ Daily sit-ups and push-ups
~ The sudden appearance of mint chocolate chip ice cream in your freezer
~ The realization of what it is you truly want to be doing with your life

Don't be alarmed. These are all good things. These new habits, desires, and bouts of clarity are signs that you are moving steadily toward that Beyond Potential Self you've been getting to know.

But I want to talk about what happens when you need (or want) to explain to the other people in your life that things are changing for you. How do you explain these subtle shifts (or in my personal case, not-so-subtle shifts) to your colleagues, friends, and family members? The process of self-redefinition is deeply personal and transformative, but as you change, those around you will inevitably react. Sharing your new self with others can be challenging, and responses may vary widely. In this chapter, we'll examine how to communicate your personal evolution to different groups, from colleagues to strangers, while maintaining your new sense of self.

Embrace the fact that reactions will differ. Some people will celebrate your growth, while others may feel threatened, confused, or dismissive. Understanding this can help prepare you for a range of interactions.

Your Colleagues

Colleagues often view us solely through the lens of our professional roles and may resist seeing us in a different light. Reframing your identity at work requires subtlety and tact, as workplace relationships can be sensitive. In the arts, especially in disciplines like music, dance, or drama, our colleagues are friends, too. Often those relationships begin in school, continue through university training, and you might even continue to perform together to this day.

When you make a professional change, it not only affects them in the day-to-day (you might not be performing with them anymore), but it brings into question all of the decisions you've made together through the years. It can feel like you're breaking an unspoken, sacred pact between you all that you will do this thing together, forever. You're breaking the sacred pact of instrumentalists by doing some (gasp!) conducting, breaking the sacred pact of the corps de ballet by (gasp!) choreographing a piece for next season, breaking the sacred pact of your fellow actors by (gasp!) directing the next play.

One helpful strategy can be to introduce your changes gradually. Whether your changes involve dressing better, going after a promotion or a more prestigious role, or you're taking on a different kind of work altogether, first choose a couple of colleagues you trust and feel close to, and then talk to them about your new plans or ideas. Bringing them into your inner circle and getting their support as helpful allies can make things feel easier and more organic in the long run.

Another strategy is to set some boundaries ahead of time. Decide how much you want to share about your personal and professional growth. Practice concise explanations for changes in your behavior, work style, or career direction.

The third strategy is one that comes from the world of sales: Assume the Yes. On a sales call, you dial the number, assuming the person on the other end is going to want what you're selling. You have the conversation as if you know they are interested and are going to say *yes*. It takes you off the defensive, and actually makes the person more inclined to say *yes*.

If a colleague comes up to you and says something along the lines of, "Hey, I heard you're going to be directing the next show. I didn't know you knew how to direct," you might naturally assume that they think it's a terrible idea, that you have no idea what you're doing, that you have no real directing experience, and who the hell are you to attempt to do this anyway? What if, instead, you assume the yes—you would thereby assume they were bringing it up to congratulate you and want to hear more about how you got interested in directing. More often than not, they were doing just that, and they are also about to ask you how you got the gig, because they, too, would love to direct something.

Exercise: Identifying Professional Qualities and Goals

What are some of the qualities and skills you'd like your colleagues to notice about your new self? How can you demonstrate these in daily interactions?

Quality	Demonstrated by

Exercise: Your Workplace Self

What core aspects of your identity do you want to showcase in the workplace?

How can you communicate your personal and professional growth without disrupting professional relationships?

Your Friends

Your friends may be more understanding of your new goals and plans, but established dynamics can still make it challenging. Long-standing friendships often come with expectations, and shifts in behavior or goals may need gentle clarification.

When I was in high school, the new head of the community music school I attended cut my scholarship in half. My parents explained to me that they couldn't cover the costs of all the different classes I was taking (two weekly private lessons, chamber music, and orchestra). Given the fees for each, I was given a choice. I could cut back to one lesson per week, or I could cut orchestra and chamber music. As hard as it was to give up being in the chamber group and orchestra with my friends, I was a junior in high school, and had the big music conservatories in my sights and I knew I needed the private lessons most of all.

It wasn't long before the kind-hearted director of the Chicago Youth Symphony Orchestra called me at home one evening. She had heard what happened, and was calling to offer me a full-ride scholarship to be in the orchestra and participate in their new chamber music program. It meant driving an hour downtown every weekend, rather than the ten-minute commute I was used to, but I was so grateful for the opportunity.

My best friends at my community music school were not as grateful for my opportunity. I was either too embarrassed to mention my cut scholarship to them, or it never occurred to me to do so, but apparently, the story they had settled on was that I had decided that I was too good for their groups and wanted to head to the big city for my musical experiences. It couldn't have been further from the truth, but that didn't get sorted out until we all were well out of university. Years of tension could have been saved by a little bit of vulnerability and some clarification.

In chapter 4, we talked about the importance of surrounding yourself with people who will help normalize your new behavior.

If you want to run, you should spend some time with other people who run, or at least seek out ways to stay fit. This might mean that you're spending less time than usual with your best friend, who prefers to stay at home and binge watch Netflix while eating takeout. This change in frequency and dynamic requires all of those same things: vulnerability about your desire to be more physically active and your need for the accountability of a running buddy, reassurance that your friendship with them remains as important to you as ever, and clarification that you won't be available to hang out and watch *Gilmore Girls* reruns on Sunday afternoons anymore, but that you'd love to find time to connect in other ways.

The important thing is to be open about why you're changing, and how you hope it will improve your life. True friends will respect your journey, but they may need guidance in understanding it. Sometimes, your changes may inspire friends to reflect on their own lives. They might feel pressure to level-up themselves, or worry that you'll move on and not want to be friends with them anymore. Emphasize that personal and professional growth is something you're committed to for yourself, and not an expectation that you hold for them.

Sadly, you might have someone in your life who resents any kind of change enough to end the friendship. You might find out that a friendship you thought ran deep, was in actuality built more on a conveniently shared schedule than anything else. It's not a pleasant experience to see a friendship wane, but it's normal and healthy for people to come and go throughout different periods of our lives. Know that your truest friends will be there cheering you on, and anyone who chooses to leave is making room for all the wonderful new friends you're about to meet.

Exercise: Having the Conversation

List three ways you can bring your friends into your new life. Maybe it's through a casual conversation or a shared new activity. Reflect on what you value most in these relationships and how your friends can support the *new you.*

Exercise: Self-Reflection Questions

Which friends have shown curiosity or encouragement about your journey?

How can you set boundaries with friends who may be skeptical or unsupportive?

Your Family

Our family members often hold the most deeply ingrained perceptions of us, shaped by years of shared history. Changing those perceptions can be especially challenging, as familial roles and expectations are often rigid. For example, I was always "the cellist." Most conversations that I had with my parents, brother, aunts, uncles, and cousins from the ages of eight until forty-eight had something to do with my life as a cellist.

While my immediate family had seen the subtle changes coming down the pike for a while, the more distant relatives that I didn't see or speak to that regularly were completely shocked when I told them I didn't really play anymore. The more awkward moment came when they started to ask me what I was doing instead. At first, I would fumble through incomprehensible words and quickly turn the conversation to their latest escapades. But then I learned the art of the transitional phrase. Here are some good ones:

~ I'm still figuring that out
~ I'll let you know when I figure that out
~ I'm doing a bit of [writing/coaching/conducting]

And sometimes, depending on the person, it can be easier to lean into the part that they will understand best. People might not understand what it means for me to be a *writer*, or a *coach*, but they do understand what an orchestra is, so when I tell them that I run the Bermuda Philharmonic, this gives them a clear role to latch onto. Even though the Philharmonic is not the main part of my career.

All I can say is that your family's reactions will likely surprise you. My mother, who had sacrificed so much for so many years to give me the opportunities I had as a cellist, had nothing to say about the fact that I essentially up and quit playing after almost five decades. NOT A WORD! Finally, when she was on her literal deathbed, I asked her if it bothered her that I had stopped playing. She said, "Oh I don't care! You can do whatever you want." I suppose we often *assume* that the people who have been around us in our previous lives will feel a sense of betrayal if we change, but I learned that you should go ahead and give them the benefit of the doubt. After all, would *you* care if your brother decided to stop being a lawyer?

Letting Others Grieve Their Loss

It was probably hardest on my husband, Paul. He had grown accustomed to introducing me as, "My wife, Kate. She's a cellist." It has a glamorous ring to it, and here in Bermuda, any career outside of reinsurance is an exotic and welcome relief. I could see him struggling with what to put after "My wife, Kate." Until finally I told him he didn't need to add anything. I could just be Kate.

It wasn't just the question of introductions, though—and this might be the thing that trips your family up the most when it comes to processing your change—he loved being married to a cellist. He loved watching me perform; he loved seeing everyone applaud for me; he loved seeing me be *the star*, and he had to find ways to support me and the changes I wanted to make while also grieving his own small loss. And I had to understand that while it wasn't a loss that was going to stop him from supporting my new endeavors, it was still a loss.

As it turns out, being on stage, whether I am playing the cello, conducting, or speaking to a group of donors, is the place where I feel the most comfortable, the most *me*. That is what he loved. He loved seeing me when I was the most me. These days, he gets to see me in that state often, and when I bring the cello out for a rare cameo performance, he's thrilled.

When it comes to something you're leaving behind, whether it was generally a positive thing (like a job, career, role, title, salary) or a negative thing (like smoking, being overly sedentary, traveling to an exhausting point), consider what it is about that thing that you connected with. Which part of it is the part that you can bring with you? Smoking made you feel very cool and rebellious, very antiestablishment. Okay–in what ways are you still cool, rebellious, and anti-establishment, but without the health consequences? Having that large salary allowed your family to feel safe and taken care of, have nice cars, and take awesome memory-making vacations. In what ways can you still provide a feeling of safety and security, and make important family memories, without the previous salary?

Family dynamics require respect, but *not* at the expense of your own identity. It's important to communicate openly, but without seeking approval. Understand that family members may take longer to accept changes, especially if they felt a particular tie to your previous identity. Those reactions are part of their own personal narratives, and giving them some space and time to sort through those adjustments can go a long way in helping them get there.

Exercise: Having the Family Conversation

Prepare a script or outline of what you'd like to say to your closest family members or partner about your decisions, goals, or changes. Start by expressing gratitude for their role in your life, while clarifying why this change is important for you.

Exercise: What Stays the Same?

Identify what it is about your previous role or identity that family members might have a hard time letting go of. How will those things remain present even as you make changes? How can you reassure them that those qualities will remain constant, no matter what?

Your New Work Contacts

New contacts in your professional sphere provide an opportunity to present the *new you* without the baggage of old assumptions. With these new acquaintances, you can create an authentic first impression that aligns with your re-defined self. There are no awkward or tricky conversations to be had about how you were previously this one thing, but now you're doing this other thing—no having to explain why, or what made you decide to, or how it's going. When you meet them and tell them you're a director, no one is likely to say, "Oh yeah? Well, since when? How good are you?" More often than not, they'll just smile and say hello, and you can all get down to work.

It can feel liberating and free to walk into a room of new colleagues and simply introduce yourself in your new identity. Your friends might give you a hard time for declining a Saturday morning brunch date in order to get a training run in because you never used to miss a brunch date, but your new running group will be happy to see you, their new running buddy. They know nothing of your previous habits.

You should be prepared, however, to introduce yourself in a new way. I definitely stumbled the first few times I had to introduce myself to a new group of people after I retired from being a cellist. "I'm a cellist," suddenly felt like a lie, but I hadn't quite figured out what to say instead. "Well, I write a bit … and I have some coaching clients … oh, and I have some group programs … and I direct the Philharmonic…." It would come out garbled and disjointed and comically incoherent. Nobody knew *what* the heck I did—including me!

Figuring out my anchor statement (chapter 6) helped, and each time I had to introduce myself, it got easier and easier. But I wish someone had told me at the time to take a moment and craft (and practice!) a new introduction. So I'm telling you: Take a moment to craft (and practice!) a new introduction. It can reflect the small steps you are taking. For example, "I'm working on my performance skills with the aim of moving from the amateur to the professional level as a pianist," or, "I'm a budding writer, working on my blog and publishing an article here and there."

Or, you can go bold and say, "I'm a pianist," or "I'm a writer."

Depending on the situation, you might want to include something short about your previous life if it pertains in some way. If I'm meeting someone for the first time as the head of the Philharmonic, I might include something like "I'm a former professional cellist who …" because that experience as a professional cellist lends credibility to my role with the orchestra. The most important thing is to be *intentional*. Approach new networking and professional introductions with clarity about who you want to be seen as now—even if you feel you are still growing into that person.

Exercise: Crafting Your New Introduction

Write a short, two-sentence introduction that reflects your current identity and values. You can refer back to the anchor statement you crafted as part of your overall mission statement back in chapter 6.

My name is _____

I am a _____

Practice saying it until it feels natural, so you can easily share it in professional settings.

Exercise: Self-Reflection Question

What specific qualities do you want new contacts to remember about you?

_____

_____

_____

The Value of Strangers

In the summer of 2009, I spent a month volunteering at an orphanage in Morocco. I was living with a group of fellow volunteers from all over the world, and from all walks of life. It was the first time since I was five years old that I would be away from my cello for more than a week, and I decided to see how it felt to explore the other, *non-cellist* parts of me. I had been *a cellist* 24/7 for thirty-four years at that point, and I was ready for a change.

Even in the brief first-day introductions, we were asked to say our names, where we were from, and why we wanted to volunteer. We weren't asked to say what we did. Suddenly, I was just "Kate from Boston," no more, no less. The person I was sharing a room with was a lovely woman named Susan, whose wealthy family had fled Iran during the revolution. She had never worked a day in her life—just traveled around the world doing volunteer work—and she was far more interested in my conversational skills than my profession.

So, I got to spend a month trying on different *non-cellist* parts of myself. What colors did I like to wear when I wasn't dressed head to toe in concert black? What food did I like to eat when I wasn't grabbing whatever was available between gigs? Who was I when I wasn't a cellist? It was mind-opening and freeing, and an experience I will never forget.

Interactions with strangers provide a unique opportunity to "try on" your new identity without repercussions. This can be a low-stakes environment to gain confidence in your new skin, and to experiment freely. You can use these interactions with strangers to practice embodying your new self, free from judgment or expectation—or, as in the case with a new work contact—the need to be at all consistent about it. With strangers, there's no need for extensive explanations. You are free to embrace your identity without apology or justification.

Exercise: The Beyond Potential Self Elevator Pitch

Imagine meeting a stranger who asks, "What do you do?" Craft a brief, authentic response that feels exciting and true to your Beyond Potential Self. How would they introduce themselves?

Re-defining yourself is a continuous process, and will change and morph as you go along. As you encounter various reactions, remember that each conversation is an opportunity to reaffirm your commitment to living your most authentic life. Some relationships may shift, others may strengthen, but your only responsibility is to stay true to your own growth.

Exercise: Self-Reflection Questions

- How does it feel to *not* default to your previous way of introducing yourself?

- How does it feel to introduce yourself to someone who has no prior knowledge of you?

- What aspects of your new identity feel easiest to communicate in these interactions?

- What parts of your new identity feel most challenging to share, and why?

- Which relationships have been most supportive of your transformation, and how can you nurture these bonds further?

9

Re-Defining the Rules

Rules are not necessarily sacred, principles are.

– Franklin D. Roosevelt

Now that you have a clearer picture of who you want to grow into by re-defining your identity and direction, and you've sorted out how you can learn to interact with the people around you without defaulting to previous patterns, let's take things a step further and create some sets of "rules" that can serve as a cohesive guide for yourself and others.

You'll be creating three guides. The first is a Mission Statement, the second one is your own take on Gretchen Rubin's fantastic Secrets of Adulthood, and the third guide is a User Manual for yourself. You can give this to people who work for or with you; you can tweak it so that it suits your students/their parents. Or, you can share it with your partner. Read on. You'll see what I mean.

The Mission Statement

A mission statement is a short declaration that defines an individual's or organization's core purpose, goals, and values. It outlines what the individual or organization aims to achieve and the principles that guide their actions.

In this more personal context, your mission statement will reflect your primary motivations, guiding values, and overarching purpose in life or work (all of which we identified earlier in Part II). It will provide a sense of direction and a framework for making decisions and setting future goals.

For an organization, the mission statement serves as a unifying statement that communicates the organization's reason for existence, its target audience, and the value it aims to deliver, often focusing on how it endeavors to make a positive impact in the world.

A well-crafted mission statement should be:

~ **Clear and concise:** It should be easy to understand and re-member.

~ **Purpose-driven:** It focuses on core values and desired impact.

~ **Inspiring and motivating:** It often reflects aspirations and serves as a source of motivation.

For example, a personal mission statement might be, "To empower and inspire others through creativity, authenticity, and a commitment to personal growth." In contrast, a corporate mission statement might be, "To bring high-quality, sustainable products to consumers while protecting the environment."

Exercise: Creating Your Mission Statement (Part 1), The Anchor Statement

Let's bring back a few of those values and goals you identified earlier. List three of your guiding values from chapter 6:

1. _____

2. _____

3. _____

And from our previous discussion on *ikigai*, recall the following:

What you're good at: _____

What you love: _____

Who needs it: _____

And from the memories exercise (page 61: Your Favorite Moments), what were some of the words that came up for you as must-haves for you to feel fully aligned in your work?

4. _____

5. _____

6. _____

Now that we have some of the basic ingredients, we're going to create an anchor statement. This short statement lies at the heart of your full mission statement. It's comprised of the following parts:

~ **What you do:** For example, I teach methods and strategies to define and reach big dreams and goals.

~ **Who do you help/work with:** For example, I work with organizations and individuals.

~ **How you work with them:** For example, I work with them through group and one-to-one coaching programs, books, talks, and workshops.

~ **What the result of the work is:** For example, they are able to be fully in alignment with their work, fully satisfied that they are doing their best work at the best of their abilities, and live the life that they want to be living, without limitations or regrets.

Next, we'll put them together in one of the following formats. *Note:* You might need to adjust it further according to your own particular pieces.

Through [How] **I help** [Who] **to** [What] **so that they can** [Result].

For example, **Through** [my books, coaching programs, and workshops] **I help** [individuals and organizations] **to** [define and reach their biggest (and truest) dreams and goals] **so that they can** [be fully in alignment with their work, fully satisfied that they are doing their best work at the best of their abilities, and living the life that they want to be living, without limitations or regrets].

Or

I work with [Who] **to do** [What] **Through** [How] **so that they can** [Result].

For example, **I work with** [individuals and organizations] **to** [define and reach their biggest (and truest) dreams and goals] **through my** [books, coaching programs, and workshops], **so that they can** [be fully in alignment with their work, fully satisfied that they are doing the best work at the best of their abilities, and creating the live they want to be living, without limitations or regrets].

Your Turn

Who: _____

What: _____

How: _____

Result: _____

Your anchor statement: _____

_____

_____

_____

_____

_____

Mission Statement (Part 2): Add Your Personal Words

Once you have your anchor statement, you can add in some of your values and core memory words. For example,

- I always aim to create a community built on trust, safety, and compassion.

- Through my commitment to lifelong learning and professional growth, my work is informed by the latest research-backed strategies and concepts.

- In all ways, I will strive to be inclusive and equitable in order to encourage diversity of ideas, experiences, and perspectives.

Mission Statement (Part 3): Consider the Future

And then add in some future-pacing. What direction are you heading in? What is the end goal?

- In the hope of ...
- With the long-term goal of ...
- With a dream of creating ...

Okay, let's put it all together. Anchor Statement + Values and Promises + Future-Pacing

Your Mission Statement

_____

_____

_____

_____

_____

_____

_____

_____

_____

_____

_____

_____

_____

_____

Rules of Adulthood

I first heard author Gretchen Rubin talk about her 25 Secrets of Adulthood on her podcast, "Happier," back in 2018, and I thought it was the most brilliant thing ever. It was a running list of all of the big life lessons, things she had figured out the hard way, and ideas passed down to her from others. She presented tidbits like, "What I do every day matters more than what I do once in a while," and, "Turning a computer off and on often fixes a glitch."

Having all of her helpful reminders written down in a list, and keeping it handy was a wonderful source of motivation and inspiration ... most of the time. Sometimes, though, I found that I didn't really relate to some of her own personal secrets. Some just didn't apply to my life circumstances, and some I disagreed with—which is fine! After all, that was *her* list, not mine. So, I started creating my own list, and that has proven to be much more helpful. I certainly borrowed some of hers, like "You bring your own weather to the picnic." I agree 100 percent. The process of creating the list was as beneficial as having the finished product, and that's what we're going to do now.

Exercise: Create Your Own List of "25 Rules of Adulthood"

To create your own list of rules think of four general categories: 1) generational, 2) daily life, 3) challenges and breakthroughs, and 4) boundaries and self-care.

1. **Generational:** Which phrases and lessons have you heard that you find to be true and helpful? For example, one of mine comes from my father: "It's only money. You can always find a way to make more of it."

2. **Daily Life:** What are some things that you've noticed about your day-to-day patterns? Think about pet peeves you have, or basic rules of behavior that you feel strongly about that make life feel better (for example, holiday music should never be played until after Thanksgiving!).

3. **Challenges and Breakthroughs:** Think back on some difficult moments you've faced or milestones you've achieved. What lessons did you learn from those moments?

4. **Boundaries and Self-Care:** Think about potentially stressful moments, and behavior or mindset rules that would ease the burden. They can even be small things like, if you feel hungry at an unusual time of day, drink a glass of water first—you might just be thirsty.

Create your very own 25 Rules of Adulthood. Print it out and keep it near you in a place of honor so that these helpful guiding principles can serve you every day.

A "You" User Manual

The idea of creating a "personal user manual" has been popularized by several leaders in the business and tech world, particularly in recent years. The idea is to create a guide that helps others understand your working style, preferences, strengths, and quirks, thereby enhancing team communication and collaboration. But in creating one in the first place, it can help us identify our needs, preferences, and styles with deeper clarity.

While it's hard to trace the exact origin, the practice gained visibility with tech leaders like venture capitalist Brad Feld and GitHub cofounder Zach Holman, who have both shared their own user manuals publicly. This idea is also frequently used in leadership training and has been adopted in team-building exercises to encourage transparency and understanding within teams. A user manual can clarify values, blind spots, and communication protocols, ultimately creating a more productive and harmonious work (or home) environment. By sharing these insights with colleagues and family members, individuals create an environment where assumptions are minimized, and each person knows how best to interact with others. Often, we go about our work (whether it's in an office space or a rehearsal space) on autopilot, oblivious to the fact that we might be approaching tasks, communication, and feedback differently than our colleagues.

Exercise: Creating Your User Manual

Creating a personal user manual is a powerful exercise that will require you to define your unique preferences, needs, and best working conditions, and it will make it easier to communicate your style to others—both in your professional and personal lives, and set yourself up for success. Here are the nine categories, and questions for you to answer in order to create your own manual:

1. Core Values and Beliefs

- What are your top three core values?
- What motivates you deeply in life or work?
- What beliefs guide your decision-making?

2. Communication Style

- How do you prefer to receive feedback? (For example, direct and concise, with suggestions, in private, etc.)
- How do you usually respond to constructive criticism?

- What are your "pet peeves" in communication?
- What's the best way for others to communicate important information to you? (For example, via email, in person, over the phone, etc.)

3. Work Style and Productivity

- What time of day do you feel most productive?
- What's your ideal work environment? (For example, quiet, lively, background music, etc.)
- Do you work best independently, collaboratively, or a mix of both?
- How do you prefer to organize tasks or projects? (For example, lists, digital tools, visual boards, etc.)

4. Decision-Making and Problem-Solving

- How do you approach decision-making? (For example, quickly, analytically, collaboratively, etc.)
- What helps you when you're stuck on a problem?
- How do you handle ambiguity?

5. Stress Management and Emotional Needs

- What signs indicate you're feeling overwhelmed or stressed?
- What helps you manage stress? (For example, exercise, alone time, venting to someone, etc.)
- How can others support you when you're stressed?
- What are non-negotiables for your mental well-being?

6. Learning and Growth

- What's your preferred way to learn new skills? (For example, hands-on, reading, observing, etc.)
- What are you most interested in learning about?
- What helps you grow and develop?

7. Boundaries and Limitations

- What boundaries do you need others to respect? (For example, time, personal space, workload, etc.)
- Are there certain times or situations when you're unavailable?
- What are deal-breakers for you in personal and professional relationships?

8. Celebration and Acknowledgment

- How do you like to celebrate achievements?
- What kind of recognition or acknowledgment resonates with you most?
- What accomplishments are you most proud of?

9. Quirks and Personal Preferences

- Are there any unique quirks or routines that are part of your daily life?
- What are your pet peeves?
- What little things make you feel appreciated?
- Is there anything you wish more people understood about you?

You'll want to review and update your user manual periodically as your needs and self-understanding evolve. By writing this guide, you can better communicate your needs, preferences, and expectations and help others understand your personal "rules" and boundaries, making interactions smoother and more supportive. Your Beyond Potential Self would be impressed.

10

Re-Defining Your Goals

It is not possible to run a course right when the goal itself has not been rightly placed.

– Francis Bacon

You've re-defined your values, homed in on what really matters, and shed some of the old expectations about who you're supposed to be. You've gotten clearer on what lights you up, and you've taken steps toward bringing those things into focus. But here's the thing: insight without direction can end up feeling like you're standing at a crossroads without a map.

The next step is to take everything you've uncovered about your purpose, your values, and your vision and turn it into a set of goals that are real, motivating, and most importantly, yours. This isn't about setting safe goals that keep you comfortably within your known limits. It's about setting goals that stretch you, excite you, maybe even scare you a little—all so that the vision you've been piecing together of your Beyond Potential Self can become reality.

In this chapter, we'll move from rethinking your foundations to defining a clear set of goals to guide you forward. We'll look at the art of setting goals that don't just get you closer to *more*, but closer to *meaningful*. By the end of this chapter, you'll have a list of goals that not only fuel your ambitions but ground them in the life and legacy you're creating for yourself.

With your new understanding that the possibilities for you are endless, we are going to identify and prioritize both your short- and long-term goals, align them with your values, purpose, and *ikigai*. We are going to make sure you're setting them in the best, most achievable way, putting some milestones in place, figuring out your personal success metrics, and committing.

Identifying Your New Goals

What are those big dreams you've locked into? What seems possible now that didn't seem possible before you picked up this book? You might have several goals and changes that you've laid out for yourself at this point, but I want to keep things focused right now. Once you understand the process, it's a rinse-and-repeat exercise for all of your goals.

The first step is to identify those Big Dreams, which are different from your goals. The Big Dreams are the endgame—those lofty, perfect ideals that you hope to (and will!) achieve. These are things like:

1. Achieve financial success as a top-tier artist, with my works purchased and sought after by the best museums and galleries in the world.

2. Win the Ironman World Championship.

3. Become completely fluent in Spanish, to the point of being able to travel and converse freely, give speeches, and write papers in the language without assistance.

Exercise: Choosing Three Big Goals

For now, I'd like you to choose three Big Goals that are on the way to those Big Dreams. Accomplishing these Big Goals will get you one significant step closer to the Big Dream. These are the first goals you want to work toward in the coming weeks and months. They can be whatever you'd like, but if you're having trouble choosing, try going for one that is related to your work/career, one that is about building a new habit, and one that is about learning or improving a skill. That might look like:

1. Create my first solo show.

2. Train for a half-marathon.

3. Learn enough Spanish to be able to have simple conversations while in Barcelona this summer.

Three Big Goals that will get me closer to my dream Beyond Potential Self are:

1. _____

2. _____

3. _____

Align Your New Goals with Purpose and Values

Simon Sinek's 2009 book, *Start With Why*, is about the difference in behavior that stems from manipulation (that is, you do the work because that's the only way you'll get paid; work better and faster, and you'll get paid more) as opposed to behavior that originates from inspiration (that is, you do the work because you believe it is helping those who need it; work better or faster, and more people benefit from it). Sinek's idea was that we should start with the *why* of what we do (or want to do, in our case) and from there, figure out the *how*, and then move on to the details of the *what*.

For many high achievers—like in the case of an artist who wants to be financially successful and in all of the world's top museums—it's going to be incredibly important to figure out your *why*.

An artist who truly dreams of a life jet-setting around the globe, seeing his work come alive in a museum or private collection, is very different than an artist who dreams of museums and private collectors seeking out his artwork so he work at home and spend time with his family.

Same dream. Different why.

And it's his *why* that will make all the difference in his pursuit of that same goal. One might set clear boundaries about travel and appearances from the beginning. One might not settle down in the first place.

Exercise: Capturing the *Why*

List your three goals one more time here, and next to each one, write down your *why* as it aligns with your values and principles.

Goal	*Why*

Now you can let your *why* guide the *how* and *what* of your goals.

How would you approach learning Spanish if your goal was to be able to converse with people? It would make sense to learn some commonly used words and phrases. If you wanted to learn Spanish so that you could write papers and give speeches, however, then you should probably focus first on grammar and spelling.

If you have a goal of running because of the sense of camaraderie you see at races, then you'll probably want to join a running group for your training period. However, if you love running and triathlons because you aren't really into team sports, and you like the sense of solitude, then a running group isn't going to be your thing.

Same Goal + Different Why = Different How

Once you have an idea of your *how* (for example, running group vs. solo training; a conversational learning path vs. traditional grammar), you can settle in on your *what*. The *what* is the specific actions you'll take to achieve your goal (for example, I'll download Duolingo vs. I'll sign up for a class at the adult education center; or I'll use an app to track my running progress and create a playlist of my favorite songs to listen to, vs. I'll join that neighborhood running club).

Exercise: Capturing Your *Hows* and *Whats*

Let's expand your list. Write down your goals, your *whys*, and add in your *hows* and your specific *whats* (or, at least some ideas if you don't know exactly yet).

Goal #1

How	*Why*	*What*

Goal #2

How	Why	What

Goal #3

How	Why	What

SMART Goal Setting

You've likely already heard about SMART goals—the system for making sure you're setting goals that you actually stand a good chance of reaching. Otherwise, it's not a goal, it's a wish. The SMART acronym stands for Specific, Measurable, Achievable, Relevant, and Time-bound.

"I have a goal of running a half-marathon in six months" is a SMART goal because it's *specific*: running a half-marathon—as opposed to being a famous runner—is precise. The goal is also *measurable* in that you can measure your distance and speed as you train to track your progress. It's *achievable*, assuming you can run, you have enough time to train, and you have 13.1 miles of land you can run on. It's *relevant* in that running a half-marathon is tied to the fact that you care about your health and fitness. Setting out to train for the Olympic running team when you have a completely different career, for instance, would *not* be relevant to you and your life. It's *time-bound* in that the race is in six months. You know exactly how long you have to train, how to plan out your training, and so on. Saying you want to run a half-marathon *someday* is not time-bound. There's no way to track whether you've succeeded or not because there's always another day (until there's not, but that's another story).

Take a moment now to think through each of your three Big Goals. Are they:

Specific? Measurable? Achievable? Relevant? Time-Bound?

Let's look at the original example above, our friend who wants to put on a solo art show, train for the half-marathon, and learn Spanish? The learning of Spanish is *specific* in that he wants to be able to have basic conversations. It's *measurable* in that he can track his Duolingo sessions and levels, and practice speaking with friends. It's *achievable*, assuming he has more than a couple of days before his trip, and it's *relevant* because he is traveling to a place where that skill would be useful. And, finally, it's *time-bound* because his trip is happening on a certain date.

Similarly, his half-marathon goal is very SMART. It's a specific race, he can measure his progress as he trains, he has the ability and the time to train for it, it's good for his health, and he has a set date for the race.

As far as his solo art show goal is concerned, well, he needs a bit more. It's *specific* in that it's 1) a solo art show, 2) a top gallery (hmmm … what determines that? Maybe he can get more specific there), and 3) he wants it to be in Chicago. It's *measurable* in that he can keep tabs on how many pieces he's creating for this show, and how many galleries he has contacted. Is it *achievable*? Well, he does have a solid track record of having his work shown in smaller galleries, so this is a natural (and achievable) next step for him—and it's *relevant* because he's an artist trying to expand his career in a certain direction. But it's not quite *time-bound*. As long as it's open-ended, he'll be able to procrastinate all he wants. He can put off both the making of the art and the calling up of galleries as long as he wants because there's no deadline.

This is where we often get into trouble—especially as creatives. "I want to record an album … someday." "I want to audition for a Broadway show … someday." "I want to start my own ballet school … someday." The truth is that production delays might mean that your album doesn't get released during your original timeline. Our artist might not land the gallery until a week after his timeline ended for his goal, and the logistical and financial details of the new ballet school might mean that it opens next year instead of this year. Without a clear time frame, however, you probably wouldn't have gotten as far as you did. All it means is that the gallery show happens a month later than planned. *But it happens!* The album gets released and the tour dates get shifted around, *but they happen.* The ballet school might be delayed a year, but if you hadn't started when you did, it wouldn't have opened for at least another year! There is an enormous difference between not reaching a goal because you kept putting it off, and not reaching a goal in the original timeframe.

Setting Micro-Milestones

Even with your specific, measurable, and time-bound goal, it can seem daunting to go after something that feels unachievable. When you created your SMART goals, you determined that with the right amount of time, and with a way to measure your progress, and with some consistency, it *would be* achievable. But it might not seem like it *right now.* Setting some smaller milestones along the way allows us to focus on something that *does* seem achievable. Maybe it's being able to run a mile without stopping to walk. And then the next milestone would be the ability to run for twenty minutes, then to do a 5K, a 10K, and before you know it, the half-marathon feels like no big deal.

This is essentially a micro-version of the whole process. These three Big Goals you have are significant milestones on your way to achieving the Big Dream Goals you set out for yourself. Consider this as the first mile on your way to winning the Ironman World Championship in Hawaii, the first finished piece of art that might someday be purchased by Tate Modern, the first successfully ordered cerveza on your way to accepting your Pulitzer Prize in Spanish.

Exercise: Capturing Your Micro-Milestones

For each of your three Big Goals, write down five to ten micro-milestones that you'll reach for between now and then.

Milestone / Goal 1 / Goal 2 / Goal 3

1. _____
2. _____
3. _____
4. _____
5. _____
6. _____
7. _____
8. _____
9. _____
10._____

Personal Success Metrics

Breaking our goals up into micro-milestones will give us plenty of opportunities to celebrate each win along the way. These mini successes help motivate you and propel you forward. When we have these small wins—completing part of a project, crossing off something on your to-do list, sending that intimidating email, or knocking another minute off your running time—our brain releases dopamine, creating feelings of pleasure, joy, and satisfaction. This release is part of the brain's reward circuitry and reinforces the kind of behavior that led to the win in the first place, making us more likely to repeat it in the future. High dopamine levels improve focus, motivation, and goal-directed behavior, which is why we often feel energized and ready to take on the next challenge after a win.

It's important to remember, however, that not every measure of success is tied to an external achievement. Other factors are tied to levels of fulfillment, well-being, or creativity. You might experience a week where nothing outward happens. You've sent out seven intimidating emails but you've yet to receive any responses. You've done some research into possible venues for your event, but so far, you have come up empty. Or, you've gotten yourself out for your training runs all four days this week, but you're not seeing any improvement in your speed.

It would be easy to feel down. Without that external win, or that shot of dopamine, you might be feeling less than motivated. This is where these internal factors of success come into play. While dopamine tends to win the popularity award as far as neurotransmitters are concerned, serotonin and endorphins are there helping us out, as well. Your running time didn't improve this week, but how did it feel to be out running? Were those lovely, pleasurable endorphins pumping through your veins, making you feel like a total rock star? Is the work you're doing (immediate results or otherwise) making you feel aligned with your values and overall goals? Are you feeling more connected with your wider community?

Put simply, do you feel like you're doing the work you're supposed to be doing? I can promise you that you *will* have those weeks—the weeks when you put in the hours, the effort, and the drive, and you end the week with nothing concrete to show for it. Far more often than not, that work you've just put in will lead to some major wins, but that feeling of general well-being, the feeling that our creative brains are being put to good use, is just as valid as that hit of dopamine.

Here are two of my favorite exercises for keeping tabs on these more internal forms of success.

Exercise: Daily Reflection Prompts

Use a short journal prompt to capture moments of alignment, growth, or fulfillment. Ask questions like:

- What did I do today that felt meaningful?
- How did I connect with others or with my values?
- What am I grateful for right now?

Exercise: 3-2-1 Check-in (The Work Version)

At the end of each day or week, jot down:

- Three things you're proud of (for example, actions, choices, moments)
- Two things that challenged you, and what you learned from them
- One area where you'd like to focus more attention in the coming days

Painting the Picture

This book is not about simply manifesting your dreams through your thoughts. My version requires reflection, thoughtfulness, intention, and quite a lot of hard work, effort, and consistency. However, one crucial step in your goal-setting process should be creating a very clear vision of what both the *end goal* and the *getting there* will look like.

"But Kate!" you might be saying, "What if I don't know exactly what I want my end goal to look like?" And to that I would reply, "Go with what you *do* know. You might not know exactly what kind of work you want to be doing, but you know that you want to be able to be at home more—go with that." Or, maybe you're not sure which major orchestra you'll land a job with, so you don't know where you'll be living. Go with what you do know: the orchestra, a city, what your life would look like in that job, regardless of where it is.

Visualizing the end goal reminds you of what you're working toward—especially during those weeks when it feels harder than usual. It reminds you to check in with your Beyond Potential Self— where did they end up? What are they doing? If it's possible for them, it's possible for you too. Visualizing the process or the steps you'll take to get there reinforces that new identity you created for yourself in chapter 7. Here are a few ways this works:

1. Activates Neural Pathways: Visualization stimulates neural patterns in the brain as if the imagined scenario were real. This process reinforces connections associated with successful outcomes, helping you *train* for success by mentally rehearsing each step. This technique, often used by athletes, musicians, and performers of all kinds, boosts confidence and prepares the brain to react more effectively in actual situations.

2. Improves Focus and Motivation: By creating a clear image of the desired outcome (our Beyond Potential Self), visualization provides a road map, enhancing motivation and commitment. That visual image of our future self becomes how we see ourselves in the present day, and as James Clear wrote in *Atomic Habits*, we behave in ways that are aligned with our identity. When the end goal feels tangible and familiar, it's easier to stay on track and make decisions aligned with that vision.

3. Enhances Emotional Regulation: Visualization can do wonders to reduce any stress and anxiety you have around your goal. Mentally rehearsing success or envisioning yourself managing challenges with ease helps calm the mind and primes it to handle high-stakes situations with confidence and less worry. This practice not only brings a sense of control but also cultivates resilience.

When I was a member of the New World Symphony, with a training fellowship for pre-professional musicians, they brought in Dr. Don Greene, the OG musician's performance coach, to work with us. He would have us imagine every single scenario that could pop up in an audition setting. One of the judge's phones could accidentally go off, or our instrument could suddenly go out of tune, or we could break a string. And then he'd have us visualize what we would do in all of those situations. The end result was that nothing threw us. Not only had we mentally practiced every scenario we could think of, but we had also prepared ourselves to be able to handle the ones we hadn't thought of, as well.

Exercise: Create a Vision Board

In addition to a regular practice of visualizing or mentally rehearsing yourself reaching your goals, I want you to choose one of the following formats for this arts and crafts project:

Create a vision board (yes, I know … but *it works)*. Grab a big piece of poster board or set yourself up on Pinterest. On one side of the poster board (or Pinterest board #1), I want you to find images that reflect your Beyond Potential Self post goal achievement. Maybe it's photos of the novel *Don Quixote* in the original Spanish, or someone holding up an Ironman trophy. You can choose images of whatever you want—the clothes you'd be wearing; the beautiful, clean house you'd be living in; the beach you'd be vacationing on. Anything goes. This page is a visual representation of your future life, so only add things you truly want.

On the opposite side of the posterboard (or Pinterest board #2), add images of you in the process of achieving those goals. This might be you practicing in the studio, creating art, studying your Spanish vocabulary words, going for a slow morning jog, or doing laps in a pool. Add anything that is a visual representation of the actions, habits, and behaviors you will need to exhibit in order to achieve your goals.

Make it a habit to look over your vision boards regularly. Set a text alarm on your phone to remind you, or combine it with another habit that you do automatically ("While my coffee is brewing, I will look at my vision board.").

Making a Commitment

The last step we have in this final chapter of Part II is to make a strong and clear commitment to pursuing this new life you've set out for yourself. One goal-setting power move is to announce your intentions publicly. You can post it on Instagram with the hashtag #beyondpotential ... and be sure to tag me (@kkayaian) so I can say hi and cheer you on!

Here are a few questions I always ask myself as I embark on a new challenge:

1. What do I need to start doing in order to achieve this goal?

2. What do I need to stop doing in order to achieve this goal?

3. Who do I need to *be* in order to achieve this goal?

I'm so excited for you, my friend. It's all happening now.

Next Steps

Armed with your clearer understanding of your selves: your Past Self, your Present Self, and your Beyond Potential Self, with your sense of identity, purpose, values, and principles all set to true north, and with your list of concrete, actionable goals all set to get you where you want to be, we're leaving the lands of reflection and planning and headed to the land of *doing*. Part III is all about strategic implementation. Get ready to re-ignite your life and your career.

Buckle up.

THREE

Re-Ignite

Everything You Need to Make it Happen

11

Re-Ignite Your Systems

A goal without a plan is just a wish.

– Antoine de Saint-Exupéry

In my experience as a coach, the number one marker that a client won't reach a goal is not due to a lack of motivation, desire, or effort, but *decision fatigue*. When vast amounts of effort are going into figuring out when they're going to go for a run, where they are going to go for a run, who is going to watch the kids while they go for a run, and whether to wear yesterday's dirty socks or borrow their partner's ill-fitting socks because all their clean socks are in the laundry, very little energy is left for the actual run. You can apply that to pretty much any goal:

~ Decisions around which free online logo creator to use

~ Decisions around which website theme to enable

~ Decisions around which Spanish language app to download

These might seem like small, inconsequential decisions—and for the most part, they are. Often the choices in front of us are all pretty much the same, and that's the problem. It's easy to waste a valuable hour of working time making that inconsequential decision, and when you multiply that by dozens of small decisions placed in front of you each day, it's enough to exhaust anyone.

A close second to decision fatigue is what I call "search dread." That important piece of information you were given? You wrote it down ... somewhere. Notes from the meeting with a donor? The branding colors you spent hours choosing—where did you put them? This chapter is all about organizing yourself, your thoughts, and your day-to-day actions so that you can spend less time thinking about (and looking for) the small, inconsequential things, and more time and energy on actually doing the work you've set out for yourself.

In this chapter, we're going to explore ways to avoid decision fatigue and search dread through the creation of a clear, step-by-step road map, strengthening your habits, organizing your digital life, and putting some of your oft-repeated tasks on autopilot through the use of SOPs and templates.

Creating a Road Map

The first decision fatigue buster answers the question everyone asks about every new challenge or project: "Where should I start?" In chapter 10, we talked about the benefits of breaking your goals into micro-milestones. Now, we're actually going to do it.

Exercise: Starting Your Road Map

On a piece of paper, write down one of your goals. If you find yourself wasting energy on which of your three goals to choose, pick Goal Two. Now, reverse engineer the necessary steps it will take to get there. That is, write the steps from end to beginning.

Let's go back to our artist example. Remember our friend who wants to have a solo show at a top gallery in Chicago this year? His steps might be:

16. Host and Attend Opening Reception

15. Install the Show

14. Begin Publicity and Promotion

13. Finalize Art Documentation (Photographs and Statements)

12. Create the Catalogue and Price List

11. Organize Shipping and Logistics

10. Confirm Press Materials

9. Send Personal Invitations

8. Decide Final Works to be Shown

7. Work with the Gallery on the Concept for the Show Installation

6. Begin Framing and Presentation Planning

5. Apply for Grants or Funding

4. Research and Pitch Galleries

3. Build a Portfolio of Related Work

2. Define the Theme and Vision

1. Begin Creating Some Art

That's a lot of steps, and he'll get to all of them, but instead of wondering whether he should start by contacting galleries, or start by applying for funding, or start by defining his vision, he can see the steps laid out clearly in front of him. His first step is to just start making some art. He can break each one of those steps into smaller steps and find the same direction. Even the Begin Creating Some Art step will have mini steps:

~ Decide that the Piece is Finished (At Least for Now)
~ Work on the Piece
~ Set Up Your Studio Space with All of the Materials You'll Need (Or What You Know of Right Now)
~ Choose Your Medium and Materials
~ Choose a Concept to Start With

There might be a few hours or days (or possibly even weeks) between Steps Four and Five, but that's the creative process, not the organizational one. The process we're concerned with here is knowing where to start, and starting there. If it's helpful to you, you can set a timeline for each part of the breakdown. This is useful especially if there are any hard deadlines involved. Is there a due date on that grant application? Or, does the gallery need to send the catalogue information to the printer by a certain date? While we don't want to rush the creative process here, it can be helpful to force yourself to put a limit on how long you can waffle between whether to use graphite or charcoal. Just choose one. If you end up changing your mind, start a new piece.

Building Habits and Routines (aka Systems)

I've spoken with many people who, after complaining about how they can't make any progress on their goals, balk at the idea of setting a specific time and place to work on them. "Too rigid! Too suffocating! I work better when I'm feeling inspired, and I don't know when that's going to be!" I've heard it all. But the truth is, inspiration is never going to lure you out of a warm, cozy bed in the morning, and that "freedom of schedule" doesn't seem to be working for you, does it? The truth is, if you've built the habit of showing up to the studio to work promptly at 9:00 a.m. each day, you'll have a far better chance at completing a show's worth of art. If you have built the habit of getting out the door to run four mornings a week, rain or shine, you'll have a far better chance at completing that half-marathon. If you have built the habit of sitting down at your desk to work on your Spanish for thirty minutes before dinner, you'll be chatting with the Barcelona locals in no time.

Part of the reason for this is that it takes out the decision fatigue factor of "When should I make some art?" "Should I run today or tomorrow?" or "Should I work on my Spanish tonight?" Even answering those simple questions takes time, effort, and energy, and more importantly, they will allow you to justify *not* doing it now. Our brains are hardwired for comfort and that warm, cozy bed, the video games you're playing in the living room, or the idea of doing anything other than working in the studio, going for a run, or studying your Spanish will win out every time.

Just like your computer has an operating system—a way of making everything work efficiently and effectively—you can create an operating system for your life. Rather than it feeling rigid, these systems create a dependable structure in your life that ensures that the important things get taken care of, almost on autopilot, so you can use your creative brain space for other pursuits. Most people find that the systems they put into place reduce decision fatigue and its friend, search dread, in such a way that they have significantly more time, energy, and freedom in their days.

For a deep dive into habits, I highly recommend James Clear's book, *Atomic Habits* (which I've mentioned earlier) but for our purposes, I'll share the four basic rules he talks about for turning a new behavior into a habit:

1. Make it Obvious
2. Make it Attractive
3. Make it Easy
4. Make it Satisfying

Making it Obvious

"Making it Obvious" means to keep the new habit right there in front of you as a reminder. So often I hear people say that they set an intention to do something, but then it just slipped their mind. Three days later, they remember that they were going to try to drink more water each day. Set the running clothes out on your dresser the night before your runs. Leave the art materials out where you can see them and pick them up. Put the Spanish language app on the first page of your phone's home screen. Podcaster and businessman Steven Bartlett wanted to improve his DJ'ing skills, so he took his gear out of the back guest room where it was gathering dust, and put it right on his dining room table. It was right there in front of him every time he walked from the kitchen or his bedroom to the front door, and he started picking it up and playing around with it every evening after dinner.

Exercise: Making Each of Your Three Big Goals Obvious	

Goals	*What You Can Do to Make Your Goal Obvious*
Ex: Write my novel	Ex: I can set up a writing desk where I'll see it every day.
Goal 1:	
Goal 2:	
Goal 3:	

Making it Attractive

"Making it Attractive" is an extremely fun part of habit forming. When I was trying to establish better and more consistent practice habits as a professional cellist, I decided to put some time and effort into the portion of the guest room that doubled as my practice space. I had already made it *obvious* by rearranging the furniture so my chair and music stand could be left out between practice sessions, and I bought an extra set of gear (an end-pin strap, some pencils, a metronome, etc.) so those never had to leave the studio if I was traveling or rehearsing away from home. This also reduced the odds of future search dread looking for them. But to make it more *attractive*, I found a beautiful rug at the thrift store to layer over the bland, sisal carpet that covered the room. I took a gorgeous ceramic vase and filled it with my pencils, and hung some artwork in the corner where it would be visible while I practiced. I also ordered an electric mug warmer so that my coffee would be there waiting for me, still warm, during my practice breaks. The previously generic "guest room where I practiced" became my little sanctuary—even though it was pretty much just a corner of a room. It was an attractive space that I loved being in.

Exercise: Making Each of Your Three Big Goals Attractive

Goals	What You Can Do to Make Your Goal Attractive
Ex: Run a half marathon	Ex: I can find a new running route that takes me through a nice park, and I can buy some snazzy new workout clothes.
Goal 1:	
Goal 2:	
Goal 3:	

Making it Easy

What if I told you that you only have to run for twenty minutes? You only have to do a quick twenty minutes and then you can go home. Or, even two minutes? Okay, how about you just need to run out your front door, to the end of the driveway, and then you can come back in, and get back in bed if you want. Still can't manage it? Okay—just put your running shoes on, and open and shut the front door. I'm borrowing Clear's example here to show what it means to "Make it Easy." The biggest obstacle to turning a new behavior into a habit is putting it off. Deciding you're not going to run is less about not wanting to achieve your goals, and more about not wanting to get out of that warm, cozy bed. The idea of making it easy takes out any concern over the difficulty of the task. It makes it harder to say no. Once you can get yourself into the habit of getting out of bed in the first place, you might as well just run the 5K. You've got your shoes on anyway, right?

Let's say your goal is focused on eating a healthier diet. If you're having trouble getting started, you can make it easy by just eating one apple each day. Apples are good for you, and they are fairly easy to eat. There. You've done something healthy! And the apple might have made you full enough to save that mini Snickers bar for some other time. Again, the goal here is to get unstuck, and to start doing *some* part of your new behavior consistently. If you can get the *what* to become a habit, then the duration and the intensity will follow naturally.

Exercise: Making Each of Your Three Big Goals Easy

Goals	What You Can Do to Make Your Goal Easy
Ex: Redesign my website	Ex: Open my computer, go to my website, and write down one thing I want to change.
Goal 1:	
Goal 2:	
Goal 3:	

Making it Satisfying

Finally, Clear's fourth rule of habit formation is to Make it Satisfying. This one ties into our dopamine fixes from chapter 10. If you give yourself a little reward each time you do a behavior that you're attempting to turn into a habit, your brain is going to make you do the behavior again in order to get that reward, that dopamine hit, again. That's right: we can train ourselves the way we train our dogs. The reward can be anything that you find satisfying. A piece of chocolate? Sure, why not? But it could also be a walk with a good friend after you spend some time studying for those exams, or a soak in a hot bubble bath after your long weekend training bike ride, or a glass of sangria after meeting up with your Spanish language conversation group. The possibilities are endless.

Exercise: Making Each of Your Three Big Goals Satisfying

Goals	*What You Can Do to Make Your Goal Satisfying*
Ex: Create a solo art show.	Ex: I will donate $1 to my favorite charity for every hour I spend working on my art.
Goal 1:	
Goal 2:	
Goal 3:	

Tracking Your Progress

You'll remember that one of the rules of setting SMART goals is that they are measurable, and you have figured out at least one aspect of your three Big Goals that you can measure. Let's talk about how you're going to measure it. There are three main formats for tracking goals:

1. Using a Journal: Whether it's digital or handwritten, use a journal to keep track of your daily or weekly progress. Either way, I would separate it from any other part of the journal. You don't want to have to wade through pages and pages of random morning pages to find your stats from eight days ago. If it's a paper journal, you can use

the pages at the very back (or the very front), or for either a paper or a digital journal, you can write the stats at the top of each entry. For example, "Saturday, May 9. Sunny skies. Hit level 4 in Duolingo last night!"

2. Use an App: I like Streaks, but Notion, Todoist, and Habitica are also good apps for gamifying your progress for you, and they do a great job of hounding you to death with guilt-inducing notifications. Trust me, you *will not forget* that you said you'd do fifty sit-ups every night before bed. Five stars, highly recommend.

3. A Visual Tracker: This can be hand-drawn on a poster board that you pin to the wall, or it can be a spreadsheet. The problem I used to have with spreadsheets is that I would go to great lengths to set them up, and then I would forget they were there. Now, I have a set time every Friday that I update my tracker and do other administrative tasks (Process, System, Habit, √).

Organizing Your Storage Drive

I mentioned search dread—that demoralizing feeling of knowing you have that important file you need right now ... *somewhere*, but exactly where is a mystery. This can happen for various reasons:

~ You work in different locations (office *and* home, or studio *and* living room *and* dining room, *and* sometimes the kitchen).

~ You use multiple storage apps or devices (you have Dropbox and Google Drive, or multiple accounts for one or the other, and there's also an external hard drive somewhere, right? Right!).

~ You have ten different notebooks and journals going at any given time—I know, they are *so* pretty!

Let's consolidate:

- ~ Different work locations: Cloud storage is key, so what you need is with you no matter which space you're in. For the remote workers who want to make sure they're using each and every room, have one space in your house be your central command HQ (if possible), and make sure everything goes back in that space at the end of each day—ideally back to its rightfully designated spot.

- ~ Multiple storage systems: For my friends with the multiple storage systems, I can tell you from experience how freeing it is to consolidate and organize them. I think I've gained about three extra hours in each week since consolidating. Once you've chosen one storage system (and again, it doesn't really matter, there are pros and cons of each, so don't spend too much time here), you're going to have to download everything from the one you don't want to use and upload it into the chosen one. Dedicate a full weekend day to it, or do a couple of files a day. It doesn't matter. It'll get done.

- ~ From there, create your folder structures. Develop a clear folder hierarchy for easy navigation. Think as big as possible here. You want to open up your storage system and see no more than six folders. For instance, mine are LLC, Executive, Financial, Personal, Operations, and Archive (always give yourself an archive folder). Everything else gets nestled into smaller and smaller folders. My podcast, for instance, has a folder within the LLC folder, and within my Podcast folder, I have a folder for each season, and inside my Season 1 folder, each episode has a folder with the episode number and title, where I keep my transcript, show notes, cover art, bio and headshot of my guest (if there was one), and the audio file. If everything in your life is organized this way, you will never suffer from search exhaustion again. I promise.

~ Multiple notebooks: If you love to process things in longhand, there's no need to change. This isn't about digital systems being superior to paper systems, but as a recovered notebook junkie myself, here are a few things that have helped.

1. Intentionality: Get out of the habit of grabbing whichever notebook is closest. Give each one a job, and it is only allowed to do *that* job. Your morning pages notebook cannot be used for work meeting notes, for example. And your planner isn't a great place to jot down someone's contact information.

2. Brand Loyalty: To the best of your ability, try to keep your various notebooks to the same brand for each job. I use the same planner year after year, and the same spiral bound notebook for my morning pages. It makes it a lot easier to catch yourself if you're about to grab the wrong one. It also makes them easier to store, and they look a lot better on your desk, shelf, etc.

3. Contact Information: Those email addresses, passwords and login information, a person's name that you should reach out to, an address, all of those short bits of information that you write down "wherever" tend to get lost, and you'll know you wrote it down ... *somewhere*, and then you'll spend the next hour looking through all ten of your notebooks. Instead, keep sticky notes on your desk, or use your notes or Notion app on your phone titled "Random Info," and put it in there. Then, when you have a moment, transfer that information to where it should live—which is the most obvious place you'd look for it.

Creating SOPs and Templates

Setting up a few standard operating procedures, or SOPs, can be time-consuming up front, but can save you loads of time in the long run, and help you from having to unnecessarily reinvent the wheel each time you do a task simply because you can't remember how you did it the last time. In an SOP, you are identifying the steps involved in completing a process. You can include pacing and timings such as, "Three days out, I should do X, or Upload the file to Google Drive—this might take five to ten minutes." Include anything that you would find helpful if you had to go back and do this task again in a year, or if you had to have someone else do it for the first time. You can create an SOP for anything: from organizing the household chores, to changing the oil in your car, or setting up an email blast for your event. I keep all of my work-related SOPs in the Operations folder in my Google Drive so I always know where to find them, and I can easily share them with my virtual assistant. I also use a consistent naming system so they are easy to pull up with a search (for example, SOP–Podcast Production or SOP–Client Onboarding).

Like an SOP, templates can be a huge organizational time-saver. In fact, I use templates for several of my SOPs. For instance, I have an SOP for sending out proposals, and within that SOP is a link for an email template, as well as a link to the spreadsheet I use to track responses, dates, etc. Everything needed to complete that oft-repeated task is laid out and linked together in one document.

Establishing effective systems, processes, and habits is the foundation of a well-organized and productive workflow. By reducing decision fatigue with clear, step-by-step plans, you'll be freeing up mental energy for more meaningful work. Organizing your digital files keeps everything at your fingertips, minimizes search exhaustion, and allows you to access the resources you need quickly and effortlessly. Developing strong habits around these systems helps turn daily tasks into automated actions, and creating SOPs and templates adds consistency and structure. Ultimately, these elements all start to work together to streamline your efforts, leaving you with room for creativity, innovation, and growth, so you can reach your goals faster and with less stress.

Exercise: Create an SOP

Choose one repeatable task related to one of your goals and create an SOP for it. First, brainstorm everything you need to do to complete that task, everything you'll need, and where those things can be found. Then, put the steps in order. Pretend you're writing out instructions for your next-door neighbor because they are going to be doing that task for you tomorrow. What do they need to know? What do they need to do? And how should they do it?

12

Re-Ignite Your Network: Gathering Your Sidekicks

The reason most people never reach their goals is that they don't define them or ever seriously consider them as believable or achievable. Winners can tell you where they are going, what they plan to do along the way, and who will be sharing the adventure with them.

– Denis Waitley

Now that you've organized yourself with habits, systems, and processes needed for goal achievement, let's talk about the people you're going to want to gather around you to ensure success. Going a step beyond the new associations we talked about in chapter 4, these are your trusted sidekicks, if you will, the ones who will help you, challenge you, make you laugh, believe in you, and encourage you in five specific ways.

Making any kind of big shift in your life can feel daunting. Whether you're attempting to level up the kind of work you're already doing, pivot into a different field, or embark on a whole-life transformation into your most ideal self, having the right people alongside you can make all the difference.

It takes guts to make these changes, and it takes perseverance to battle *imposter syndrome* and overcome truckloads of self-doubt. There will be moments when it seems like it's not working, or that it's not even worth it, and there will be moments when it feels tedious and boring. Author and marketing expert Seth Godin referred to this feeling as "the Dip." Let's say you've been plugging away at it for a while, but you haven't quite seen any results. You've burned through the initial high of new project euphoria, and discovered that aspects of it are not always easy or fun. It's enough to make anybody quit. The truth is that most people do quit. This work requires resilience, and grit, and it requires that you not attempt to do it on your own. We need to get your support system in place.

There are five different roles you'll want covered by your sidekicks, and I'll take you through each of them. To borrow from a classic example, you'll want to have your Obi-wan, your Yoda, and you'll definitely need a Chewbacca, otherwise you have a significantly lower chance of making it to the other side.

The Proof

It's easier to motivate ourselves to take on something scary if we know it will work out. Being able to point to an example of someone who has done something similar definitely helps in that regard. As soon as you start to hear your inner voice say something rude like, "That's a dumb idea; you could never get away with doing something like that," you can point to that person, colleague, or celebrity and say, "Well, they did it. So, I might be able to do it too." They are your Proof.

You can also model your steps after them. Find out what steps they took, and then try following those same steps yourself. If it worked for them, it would probably work for you too. Our half-marathon friend can find people who have run half-marathons and ask them how they trained.

It's easier to find proof in our everyday network of friends and colleagues when the goal is a standard one. There are millions of people who run half-marathons every year, for example. Chances are, you know at least five of them. It gets a little bit trickier when you want to do something that's brand new. How do you find proof that it's doable, if no one has ever done it before?

When I wanted to start an online summer festival in 2020, such a thing didn't exist yet. There wasn't an example of an online summer music festival that I could point to and model mine after, but I had been to enough summer in-person festivals over my lifetime, and I had seen people put together online conferences and summits, so I just combined the two. You can do something like that too, if no one has done exactly what you want to do. Find people who have done similar things, and then put your own twist on it. There are likely to be big commonalities when it comes to the nuts and bolts of your unique goal. Building a website looks pretty much the same no matter what the industry is, for example.

If you want to run a half-marathon barefoot in Siberia (hopefully in the summer), then you can find people who have run half-marathons barefoot, and you can find someone who has run in Siberia (there must be one, right?).

You can also find your proof in someone you don't know personally. There are plenty of young athletes who watch the Olympics and suddenly their dreams seem possible too. Is there a celebrity or someone outside of your orbit who has done what you are looking to do? What can you find out about their process online? Maybe they've written an autobiography or given enough interviews that you can distill their entire step-by-step method to get where you want to go.

Exercise: Who is Your Proof?

Look around you. Who do you see that you can use as your Proof? Write their name on a piece of paper and pin it to your workboard and, without getting all creepy about it (please don't do that), find out what you can about how they did it.

Can you think of one person for each of your three Big Goals? Or, is there one person who is proof of all three?

One person who serves as Proof that what I want to do is possible is:

_____

Something I can do to figure out how they did it is to:

_____

The next time I hear "I could never do that," I will:

_____

The Peer

And, yes: They all start with the letter P. It's easier to remember that way. A Peer is someone who is going through a similar journey/path/transformation—insert any of those grossly overused words one can use to describe the hard work of getting yourself from Point A to Point B—as you. Ideally, this peer is starting from the same or similar Point A and is looking to get to or near the same or a similar point B.

This is your equally out-of-shape buddy who is going to train with you to do the race; your childhood friend, who is already a veteran marathon runner is a mentor, a trainer, a guide, your Proof perhaps, but they are not your Peer. Not yet, anyway.

Your Peer is someone who also wants to make some kind of career or life pivot. It could be similar to yours. For example, you both want to start a chamber music festival. Or, they could be wildly different, like you each want to shift into a different career altogether. The point is that they are as giddy and excited about it as you are, and also a bit apprehensive, a little terrified, and sometimes want to throw up at the idea of changing things up, too.

They will walk the walk and talk the talk with you. When you're having a great day, they will rejoice in your wins, and when you're having a lousy day, they'll commiserate with you. It's hard. They get it. They'll remind you that it's worth it. And you'll do the same for them.

In the coaching world, we call that "jumping in the pool with you." If you get in the pool and the water is freezing, the coach will help gently guide you to the ladder to get out of the proverbial pool, or help you reframe it as "refreshing!"—whatever's most helpful to you in the long run. But a Peer? They will jump right in with you, and say, "Oh, yeah—this is freezing!"

One of the things I hear most often from clients who are reaching out to me for the first time is that they feel very lonely and isolated in their desire to make such a big change. They worry that their colleagues and friends will at best, just not get it and, at worst, completely snub them.

And they might be right.

The person who is trying to be healthy and kick some bad habits might meet up with their friends, who give them a hard time for ordering a seltzer and a salad instead of a Malbec and manicotti. I'm not saying they shouldn't hang out with those friends, but it would be a lot easier if they were all trying to be healthy together and all toasting with pomegranate La Croix.

When I decided to start working with a business coach, what appealed to me the most was the group of people I would be working alongside. That group of people, all of whom were working on their own projects, became my rock. We took turns alternating between tears of frustration and stories of victory, and having a space where I could be 100 percent real—to not have to hide what I was working on, or be shy about my wins, was a big part of my success.

In my own group programs, like Creatives Leadership Academy and Profit Pivot, I aim to create the kind of atmosphere that fosters those connections—choosing participants who will benefit from and enhance each other's work. But the alchemy of each cohort always takes on a life of its own as peers build connections and trust between them. Even my one-to-one clients get to come to my weekly office hours, so that they too can meet some of their peers—those people in their shoes who are experiencing similar things. It makes such a difference. If you can surround yourself with a whole group of them, you'll have won the lottery, but you'll feel a big difference even with one Peer.

Exercise: Who Are Your Peers?

When it comes to each of my three goals, these are some people I consider my Peers:

Goal #1: _____

Goal #2: _____

Goal #3: _____

If I can't think of any who I know, I could probably find some here:

_____

_____

_____

The Pillar

As I mentioned, I have made a couple of big pivots in my career. The first was when I left the freelance orchestra world in Boston and started touring around and doing more solo performances, and the second was when I left my performance life behind altogether and moved into online teaching and coaching.

I remember some serious low points in the early days of each case, like that concert in Seattle that was attended by … five people? Or, the time I had a memory slip in the last movement of a Bach Suite I had played a gazillion times? Or, that time I showed up to perform on a "concert series" at a wine bar, and it turns out it was just a bar with live music. Let's just say they were *not* expecting Bach. Or, that time I had the final "graduation session" planned for my first big coaching group and there was an explosion at the power station twenty minutes before, which put the entire island into a blackout. Or, the numerous times I sent out a wrong email, posted the wrong dates, or an expert I hired gave a total dud of a class. I could go on and on.

I'm going to let you all in on a little secret. This whole career pivot thing? Not every day is going to be an awesome day. The only way to get good at something new is to screw up and learn from your mistakes. But those days feel hard. What's your secret weapon in those moments? The Pillar.

The Pillar is the person who holds you up, who keeps you from crumbling in the middle of a launch when you round the top of the curve of the rollercoaster and start barreling headfirst toward the ground because the power was cut. Spoiler alert—it'll all work out; it just might not feel like it in that exact moment.

Your Pillar can be your spouse, your best friend, your mom, your kind neighbor who thinks you're the bomb, or your Aunt Susie (who always seems to know just what to say to make you feel better). At times, I act as a Pillar for a client who needs one. Just standing there, supporting them as they do courageous things on difficult days makes a huge difference.

Your Proof? You might not even have met them. Your Peer? They're going through the same thing. You can cry on their shoulder, but they're probably crying on yours as well. Your Pillar, though? They are there for you. Strong, always encouraging, always on your side. When you are on top of the world, they tell you they believe in you. When you're ready to quit, they tell you they know you can do it.

When I was growing up, doing the whole monkey dance of competitions and auditions that all young musicians go through, I would get incredibly mad when, after a not-exactly-my-best-most-shining-moment performance, my dad would come up to me, beaming, and say, "That was terrific, honey! You were the best one!"

I would get so annoyed because a) he was clearly wrong, and b) he didn't know anything. My friends' parents were all professional musicians. They knew. And they could be honest about their kid's performances. They could go home and critically break everything down and do a full SWOT analysis of that day's performance.

And there I was with my dumb dad—what the heck did he know? I could have walked out on stage with a broken cello, and he would have told me I was great. In hindsight, I was the luckiest girl around. He was such a gift. He was my first Pillar.

The truth is that we all desperately need someone like him in our life—someone who, no matter what, supports us. The person who believes in you, your dreams, and your ability to make them happen. The person who will run errands and take on extra chores for you when you need to work a few extra hours a few weeks in a row. The person who is blind to (or will, at least, kindly ignore) your bad moments and consistently tells you to keep going, that you're doing great.

These days, my Pillar is my husband. He's a scientist, and he had to google *cello* the night we met just to see which instrument it actually was. For years, he would feel bad that he couldn't talk to me seriously about classical music, or my work, the way I could with my colleagues, and eventually I was able to convince him that I didn't need that from him. In those colleagues, I had my Peers—which was important, but only one *P* out of the five. He was my Pillar, my source of strength and support, and I didn't need him to know a damn thing about my industry for that.

Those "terrible days" will sort themselves out. The mistakes will get fixed or rectified, and you will learn everything you need to know. All your Pillar needs to do is stand there, allowing you to lean on them for a little bit.

Exercise: Who is Your Pillar?

The person who supports me no matter what, and is a source of strength for me when I need it, is:

_____

_____

The Professor

The other day, I got a nice surprise email from an acquaintance from Boston. This woman was a regular at my concerts. She was not a cellist herself, but a huge fan, and she always talked about how she wished she could play. She was well-educated, and after an impressive career in the corporate sector, she retired early and did even more impressive things. But she had always dreamed of hosting salon evenings in her swanky home and playing Brahms' Piano Trios into the wee hours of the morning. In her email, she excitedly told me that she had decided to make learning the cello her next project.

I was so happy for her, and asked her who her teacher was. It's a small community, and I was sure I would have known them. I was excited to call them up and tell them how much fun this woman would be as a student. She said, "Oh! I'm not studying with anyone yet. I'm not good enough. I'm just going to learn the basics myself and then I'll go and find a teacher.... But could you just tell me how to do vibrato real quick?"

Um.... Not really. No.

It's not that I can't teach someone how to vibrate, obviously. I did it for more than twenty-five years. It's that I can't just tell someone how to do it and then send them on their way. I don't care how many advanced degrees one holds from MIT. It involves exercises and repetition under a watchful, experienced eye. It requires feedback and adjustments. It requires information you can't get from a YouTube video.

Now, if you're merely curious about something or you just want to dabble for fun, then by all means, go for it. I'm a huge fan of hobbies. And if you're curious about what that weird shaking thing cellists are doing with their left hands, I'll happily tell you all about it. But if you want to really do it—be proficient enough to be able to play (and read) chamber music, for instance, then you simply need to work with a teacher.

Or … a Professor. It starts with the letter *P*.

If you want to get a bit fitter, then you can just do a home workout. but if you want to change how your body looks, then you'll save yourself a lot of time and frustration by signing up with a personal trainer. The same is true for preparing for orchestra auditions, learning a language, and learning a sport. For just about everything, really. Especially revamping your career. Take it from me.

Back in 2017, I knew I wanted more from my music career. I loved my teaching and I loved my performing, but the entrepreneurial itch that had followed me around my whole life was resurfacing. I did some Google searches for help, guidance, examples … anything, really. And I came up empty. So I turned to podcasts and found several that were mind-blowing to me at the time. They were mostly podcasts by online marketing and business leaders like Amy Porterfield, Jenna Kutcher, and Steph Crowder.

I was hearing terms that I, as a musician, had never heard before: ROI, conversion, launching, email marketing platforms, algorithms, Ideal Customer Avatars, and landing pages. My head was spinning. But I was fascinated. I knew that as a musician, if I could harness the business side of things—things I never learned in music school, I could, in fact, do a lot more. So I stuck with it, and I learned a lot. I felt on top of the world.

These people were masters. They were my teachers. But as I dove into their content, I kept noticing a common theme. One after another, they would at some point refer to their business coach....

Their *what?*

All of these business leaders had business coaches. And they all swore by them. So, I was determined to get one, as well.

One of those podcasters, Marie Forleo, had a digital course called "B-School," and I signed up for it. It wasn't cheap, and I didn't have a ton of extra cash lying around, but I decided to invest in myself. Marie Forleo would be my business coach, even if she didn't know who I was. I learned more lingo. I learned how to do a few more things. And there were thousands of other people in the course wanting to network and exchange information.

But none of them were artists. And I felt very alone.

My niche of classical music was a strange one. Every time I went into a live Q&A and asked something about my projects, I was met with blank stares. They just weren't quite sure how to deal with my niche. So I kept looking. I was determined to find someone who understood both the business *and* the industry.

Eventually I found that person in my first coach, Jennifer Rosenfeld, and as soon as I started working with a teacher who was well-matched to who I am and what I wanted to do, doors started to fly open for me. Because just like vibrato, you can't just read a book about creating a business and do it. You need guidance in real time. You need someone there to answer questions, help steer you, and sometimes just say, "Yep! You're doing great! Keep going!"

And now I know firsthand what those podcasters were talking about, and why they have their coaches. While I now have the experience and knowledge to be able to guide my own clients toward their goals and help them achieve their dreams, I, too, will have various coaches in my cheering corner for the rest of my career. They are my Professor*s*, teaching me the things I want to learn more about, and helping me improve my work.

And it's funny how similar the conversation is when someone attempting a big career shift says to me, "Well, I think I can completely overhaul my career on my own for now, but could you just tell me how to do X?"

Um.... Not really. No. Not in five minutes. For that, you'll need a Professor.

Preferably this will be someone with a proven track record, who has experience doing what you need to do. If you are just starting out and dabbling, maybe that person is a podcaster you're listening to. Or, maybe you'll dive into some of those inexpensive digital courses that teach you how to do one thing or another.

But eventually, if you truly want to succeed, you're going to need to bring in the big guns. The Professor can help save you months of procrastinating and frustration. They can keep you from making costly mistakes and they can help you get to where you want to go.

Exercise: Who Are Your Professors?

People who could help me develop the skills I need to achieve my goals are:

Goal #1:

_____

_____

Goal #2:

_____

_____

Goal #3:

_____

_____

The Prodder

Last but not least, we have the Prodder. The Prodder is the person in our lives who nudges us (physically or mentally) to Get. It. Done. The person who will ask, "Have you done your practicing yet today?" or "Did you send those emails this week?" This person must be selected by you. If they have selected themselves for this role, we tend to call them The Nag, which is less helpful to our progress.

While being surrounded by a strong peer group can help with a sense of accountability, and you might want to look good for your Professor by always doing what they have suggested, I would strongly suggest asking just *one* person to be your Prodder.

For me, I chose someone from my first coaching program. My Prodder and I check in with each other every single day, and tell each other what we are committing to for that day. Some of the prodding is an encouraging, "You can do it, Kate! It's going to be great!" and some of it is a stern reminder, "You said you wanted to do five each week—how many more do you need to do?" I do the same for her. Although she is my Peer, as well, she's not necessarily going to jump in the pool with me and say, "Oh, I know! You've had such a week! You should totally take the rest of the day off!" Nor is she going to coach me out of a bad decision. She's simply going to remind me what I said I was going to do. She's going to give me the gentle, yet prodding nudge that I need to get it done.

Exercise: Who is Your Prodder?

Someone who would be a good Prodder, or Accountability Partner, for me is:

_____

_____

Your Five-Person Support Team

Your five-person team is your Proof, your Peer, your Pillar, your Professor, and your Prodder.

Is there an overlap in these five people? Sure, sometimes. The more successes my peers rack up, the more they become my proof. At times, my peers will prod me into action. My professors (coaches and trainers) have at times shown that they are also peers as they work through their own career issues (which is amazing, by the way, to follow along in real time as they tackle real-life problems I'll someday face). And at times they have also prodded me. And my prodder is also a peer, and sometimes we both have days where we look at each other and say, "This all feels hard today … but let's do it anyway."

Although the lines sometimes get blurry, the fact that I can state with full clarity who fulfills each role in my life has made all the difference.

~ If I ever start to question whether I can do the things I want to do, I look to my Proof—the people out there doing incredible things each and every day, despite similar odds.

~ When I want to commiserate or share a win without feeling like I'm bragging, I have the Peers in my mastermind group. They make a pretty amazing cheering squad.

~ When I need support, which in my case usually means I need someone to pick up groceries *and* cook dinner, *and* do the dishes afterward, I have my incredible husband, my Pillar, Paul.

~ When I need to learn how to do something, want help shaping a new idea, or want guidance into what my next steps could/should be, I have my coaches, the Professors.

~ And when I find myself wanting to procrastinate, I have my Prodder to hold me accountable.

Exercise: Your Five-Person Support Team

Name the people on your support team.

Proof:

_____

Peer:

_____

Pillar:

_____

Professor:

_____

Prodder:

_____

As creatives, we tend to grow up believing it is *all* on us: Whether or not we have the drive and ambition to get our butts into the studio; whether or not we have the talent and skills necessary to *make it*; and whether or not we have the right personality to get into the *right* circles. We are taught that it is on us alone, as individuals.

But really, it's about the team. Always has been, always will be. And whether you are a student, a teacher, an amateur, or a professional, once you figure this out and get your team in place, there is no limit to what you can accomplish.

13

Re-Ignite Your Self-Mastery: The Five Levels of Internal Growth

What lies behind us and what lies before us are tiny matters compared to what lies within us.

— Ralph Waldo Emerson

I have made some big changes in my life and career, and have helped hundreds of clients make changes of their own. Some are moving into leadership positions within their field, some are expanding the reach of what they do within their field, and some are changing fields entirely. And with most of those big career-based changes comes a few life changes, as well. As you are finding out for yourself, it's all connected: the work we want to do, the life we want to live, the relationships we want to nurture. One big change often brings several smaller changes along for the ride. It's exciting, and fun, and scary, and terrifying all at the same time.

Because it requires a tremendous amount of growth.

There is a lot of talk about growth—in fact, we've made two entire genres out of growth: Personal Growth and Professional Growth. But growth is growth. It always requires the same of us: getting outside of our comfort zone, taking on a risk or a challenge, and shifting our identity.

And we all know what the result of that growth looks like, right? It could be a promotion, or getting to the next level in a job, an audition, or a sport. It could be moving from "beginner" status in a foreign language to "conversational." Or, going from couch potato to a half-marathon runner.

When we think of growth—be that our own, or in someone else—we think of the outward changes in their appearance, work status, behaviors, or even bank accounts. But more often than not, that outward change in appearance or status is preceded by a far quieter change. This first kind of growth is subtle. Sometimes it's something that as a coach, I can recognize in my clients before they see it themselves.

It's *internal growth*.

We all know that picture of the iceberg with the top part of it sticking out of the water representing external growth, and the larger portion of it underwater and unseen that had to happen first.

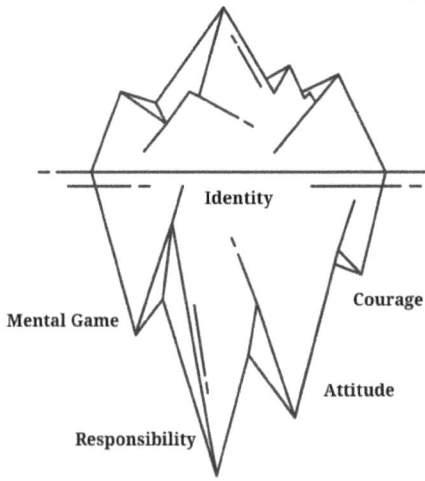

The top part could be the first sale of a new artist's work. The bottom part could be the years of wondering if they should quit their job and take art classes, or wondering if they were even allowed to, in midlife, suddenly rebrand themselves as an artist. It could be the months it took to post their work on Instagram or to show their teenagers what they had created. It could be the courage it took them to quietly submit a piece to an open call.

The top part could be the successful opening night of a singer's directorial debut, accepting the roses and applause. The bottom 90 percent could be the years of talking about it, the months of resistance, and then finally getting that proposal written. The slow identity shift from "just a singer to singer, producer, and director." The baby steps in confidence building as one tiny courageous act made the next one ever-so-slightly less terrifying.

I've had clients who, six months into working together, put out a splashy, amazing project with loads of visibility and hype. I've had others who have worked with me for years without any outward "project" to show for it, but have, in that time, gained total clarity around what they want to do with their lives, confidence in the person they are, and belief in the person they are becoming. Tasks that were once crippling to them (like posting their work online, or sending an email to someone they want in their network) are now done regularly, without a second thought.

Those are some of my favorite coaching moments. The outward successes are fun, of course, and are cause for much celebration and acknowledgment of the hard work that went into them, but witnessing these quiet, subtle, internal moments of growth are incredibly meaningful to me. Without them, there would be no outward successes. And once this kind of internal growth occurs, anything is possible.

What was the difference between the fast clients and the slower clients? Nothing at all—the process is the same for everyone.

But sometimes a client will come to me having done some of the preliminary work on their own, or with a previous coach. But after all of the coaching I have done, experienced, and witnessed, one thing I know for sure: You won't see external results until you've done the internal work. That bottom part of the iceberg is what keeps the top part anchored. Without it, it's just a piece of ice floating around aimlessly. It'll melt, crash into other ice, and will always be unsteady.

I'm sure there are many ways to experience internal growth, but here are the five most important ones I see occurring in the months or years leading up to a big, outward success. I usually see them happening in this order, almost as if they're different levels of a video game.

Level 1: Responsibility

Sometimes it feels as though the world is against us. Your colleague always gets hired instead of you because they are dating the contractor. You won't ever get hired at that school because you haven't won any awards. Or, the gallery owner only brings in their friends to do shows, so obviously, you never get asked to show your work. Everyone around us is conspiring to keep us broke, miserable, and out of work. It's definitely not *our* fault.

I have a visceral memory of sitting on my bed one evening while in the midst of a pretty low point in my life. If I'm speaking plainly, I was deeply depressed. Life was not going the way I wanted it to be going. My love life was a disaster, my career felt hectic and disorganized, and opportunities weren't coming as quickly as I thought they would be. But one evening, sitting in my bedroom writing in my journal, I wrote these words:

"I need to stop expecting everyone else to make me happy. It's not their job. It's mine."

I don't know where that clarity of thought came from, but it came, clear as day—so clear that I still remember the exact line twenty years later. I made a list right then and there of the kinds of things, people, and work I wanted in my life—a list of what would make me happy—and then I brainstormed ways to get them. That was the moment I started to take responsibility for my own life.

Now, I see it in my clients, too. I see the shift from placing blame for their hurt feelings, seeming lack of opportunities, and financial woes on everyone around them, to taking ownership of all of it— finding intention in their reactions to people's words, creating the opportunities they want, and finding ways to generate the financial life they want. "It's so unfair!" becomes "I wonder how I can...."

Suddenly, they find easy ways around those previous obstacles.

~ They write an email to the contractor saying, "Hey, I'd love to play if you ever need someone." And the contractor replies, "Awesome! I always thought you weren't interested. Can you do our next concert?"

~ They start their own teaching program and get so much attention from it that their dream school asks them to join their faculty—even without the awards.

~ They ask that clique of artists if they'd be interested in doing a collaborative show. Before they know it, they're booked at that perfect venue.

Exercise: Reframing What's Holding You Back

What are the circumstances that you feel have unfairly held you back? If you were to take some responsibility, how might you reframe them into possible opportunities?

It's so unfair!	*I wonder how I can ...*

Level 2: Attitude

The second internal growth shift happens after we take responsibility for our lives and start to get more proactive about seeking those opportunities we want. The initial excitement of a new idea gets bombarded with all of the reasons it won't work. I refer to this kind of thinking as the *No, because ...* mindset we learned about back in chapter 2. This second marker of internal growth is when that *No, because ...* mindset turns into a *Yes, if ...* mindset.

First, we take responsibility for our lives, and then develop the mindset to get curious about how to make it all happen.

~ Yes, if we could raise the money
~ Yes, if I could find the right venue
~ Yes, if I could find the courage to record that album
~ Yes, if I could find two quiet and uninterrupted hours each day to work

Exercise: Locking into an Attitude of Possibility

Let's use that previous exercise and take it a step further. List one thing you want to do. Write out your reasons for not being able to do it, and then write the *Yes, if* ... response:

I'd really love to:

I can't because:

But maybe I could if I:

Level 3: Improved Mental Game

We've now gone from "I am responsible for my own life" to "I can do this ... if...." This third step in the path of internal growth is what separates the successful from the creative bystanders. No matter the circumstances, those pesky mindset monsters, like imposter syndrome and resistance, will rear their ugly heads.

No one is safe.

Most people will allow a single negative thought like, "People will laugh at me" to derail their progress, and sadly, their own personal and professional growth in the process. Most people will allow a week of resistance—whether your particular brand of resistance is procrastination, distraction, martyrdom, or indulging in unhealthy habits—to mean that they aren't capable of taking on this beast of a project. Or, they'll let it mean that they don't really want to do it, even though deep down, they know they do.

Imposter syndrome is our brain's way of keeping us safe within the confines of our comfort zone. Growth means stepping out into the unknown, into uncertainty, into uncharted territory. Our brain will throw any and every warning thought at us to keep us from even attempting such a dangerous thing. It's hardwired from back in the days when that uncharted territory might have included animals that wanted to kill us. But in modern days, the worst thing that can happen is more likely a slight wound to our ego, and that is not fatal. I promise.

Resistance—that inability to get yourself into the practice room when your audition is looming; the intense need to scrub the kitchen floor before you could possibly start working on that painting.; the decision that you're simply too busy caring for everyone else to work on your own project—is nothing but fear. I've talked about this before. It's always just fear: Fear that you won't be good at it, fear that you'll hate it, fear that you'll love it, but no one else will. Maybe it's fear that after all this time, it just won't go as planned.

Level-3 growth is not when you no longer face imposter syndrome or resistance, because you always will. I always will! Barack Obama, Yo-Yo Ma, and Oprah always will. As I said, it's hardwired into us—and humans haven't quite evolved out of it yet. Level-3 growth is when you can recognize it for what it is, and stare it down.

It's when you can see yourself procrastinating, and you call yourself on it. "It's okay. Just do ten minutes of work, and then you can get back to the video game," or "Yes, people might laugh—and I can handle that. I'm doing this project anyway. After all, what are they doing to put themselves out there? Maybe they don't have the guts, but I do."

If you can remember that those negative thoughts are popping up to "protect" you from "perceived risk," (and if you think of it that way, it's kind of sweet) you can say "thank you," and allow it to come along for the ride. But you're the boss, and you'll make the final decision. Just as you don't necessarily believe your four-year-old when they tell you there are monsters under the bed, you can acknowledge these thoughts and remind yourself that they're just made up.

Exercise: Recognizing Your Mindset Obstacles

What are your favorite forms of resistance? Is it procrastination? Or, procrasti-cleaning? Numbing yourself with substances, food, or TV? Taking on extra duties at home or in your community so that you simply don't have time? What negative thoughts always plague you when you're about to try something new?

Whenever I am avoiding work, my tendency is to:

_____

The unhelpful thought that always seems to pop into my head when I think about trying something new is:

_____

The next time I hear that thought, I will:

_____

Level 4: Courage

If Level-3 growth is the recognition of mindset obstacles, and the decision to overcome them, Level-4 growth is when a person finally gathers the courage to act. They write the email, they create the social media announcement. Often, they need a little bit of help crossing that finish line, and part of my job as a coach is to give them the push they need to send the email and to post the social media announcement.

Traveling up through Level 1 ("It's on me"), Level 2 ("This could work, if ..."), Level 3 ("I'm not going to believe these negative thoughts"), all the way to Level 4 takes tremendous growth, and if you can get to Level 4, you're pretty much guaranteed to make it all the way. The reason? Once you can get yourself to act with courage to do the scary thing, to stretch outside your comfort zone, you'll start to gain the confidence that comes from experience.

It's always terrifying to send that first email, to post that first piece, to ask for that first meeting. It's terrifying for every single one of us. But if you can summon your courage and do it, you might get a nice response. Suddenly, sending an email isn't so bad—maybe you could even email someone else. Next thing you know, you're "scary sending" emails to people regularly. Emails that before seemed impossible.

As a coach, I see the growth in clients who would message me previously to say, "I need to email so-and-so. What should I write?" and then (ten minutes later), "Okay, I've written the email. Do I really have to send it?" Before long, they're sending me messages that say, "So, I emailed these three people, and sent them proposals ..." like it was no big deal.

That kind of growth *is* a big deal.

Luckily for all of us, courage is like a muscle. The more we use it, the stronger it grows. You can build your own courage muscle now by trying out small acts of courage in your day-to-day life. *Small* will mean different things to different people, of course. To one person, it could be summoning the courage to tell the barista that, actually, you ordered an iced latte, not a hot one. Or, it could be calling your local politician to express your concerns about an issue in the community. Whatever it is, start using your courage muscle a little bit more every day and you'll find you're becoming more comfortable with the idea of flexing it in the big moments.

Exercise: Five Small Acts of Courage

List five small acts that could help strengthen your courage muscle:

1. _____

2. _____

3. _____

4. _____

5. _____

Level 5: Identity

I recently had a client named Julie who was making a huge shift in her career to a totally different industry. Her most terrifying moments centered around people asking her what she did. "What do I tell them?" she asked. "That I'm attempting to be a professional musician? That I am a professional musician now? What if they want to know where I'm performing? I don't have any concerts yet. I feel like a fraud."

I get it.

For forty year years I was "Kate the cellist." It's how I was introduced, recognized, and referred to. When I stopped being a cellist, I was writing daily, but hadn't published anything other than my blog, and that same question would send me into a panic. But one day, someone asked me what I did. It was someone who never knew me as a cellist. I responded, "I'm a writer," and just like that, I felt my own tremendous growth. Although they're just words, they signal reaching a place where your own identity shifts. Once I felt confident in my identity as a writer, I found myself acting like a writer—as in, writing more. I sought out opportunities to write for other people and publications. And as much as I was writing before, until I was able to lean into my own identity shift, I wasn't quite there.

This client of mine went to a reunion, and during our session a few days later, she recounted different interactions she had with old classmates. I asked what she said when people asked her what she was up to. "You know, I think I just said I was a violinist. It just sort of rolled off my tongue. It didn't feel as strange as it did before." And from that moment, she was truly on her way. She had climbed up from the underwater part of that iceberg. From there, she took herself more seriously as a bona fide musician. She started taking (and winning) auditions, approached other "actual, professional" musicians to collaborate on projects with her, and started posting videos regularly on social media. Once she had reached this fifth level of internal growth, anything became possible for her.

The actor who finally identifies as a director, and is able to communicate with people about her production idea as a director (rather than as an actor who is trying to be a director), that person is guaranteed to make that production a reality. Or, the public school music teacher who allows himself to identify as a performer and starts to see the gig offers roll in. Or, the freelancer who starts to identify as a groundbreaking pedagogue and gains the attention of major arts schools. These are the ones who are allowing themselves to lean into their new identity without embarrassment, and to reap the benefits.

Mind you, in each of these cases, while you can *see* the tremendous growth that's happened, the people in question had not actually put out their first product, project, program, or whatever they were doing. There was no external evidence of their growth. But as you can see, they had already done the hard part.

These five levels of internal growth represent the largest portion of the iceberg that's below the water. The 90 percent of taking responsibility, seeing the possibility, pushing through the negative thoughts, demonstrating courage, and allowing for that identity shift. The rest is easy. The rest is just doing the thing. Only now, you've grown into the person who can do the thing. You have all the tools you need.

Where do you fit into this video game of personal growth? Are you at Level 5 already or are you starting out at a Level 1? Are you somewhere in the middle? What do you need to do in order to get to the next level?

14

Re-Ignite Your Momentum: How to Take Meaningful Action

Make at least one definite move daily toward your goal.

– Bruce Lee

Finally—we're going to start taking some real action toward your goals, my friend! Each previous chapter of this book, as well as the exercises you've done within them, have brought you to this moment. You have reflected on who you were, who you are, and who you want to be. You have gotten to know your Beyond Potential Self pretty well by now, and set some clear goals for yourself that will get you closer to becoming that version of yourself you're dreaming of. You've learned how to organize yourself and your space, gathered the right support network around you, and have leaned into and worked through some of the internal forms of growth that are necessary for this external transformation. All that's left is to start doing it.

But how, exactly?

In the fall of 2020, at the height of the COVID-19 pandemic, I ran my first group coaching program, Profit Pivot. It was a ten-week course that would help my out-of-work musician colleagues create online initiatives that could supplement the income they'd lost due to the cancelation of performances. I ran it four times in a row, and each group was filled with highly intelligent, highly successful musicians who were used to working hard. They had ability, discipline, and drive. They wouldn't have had the careers they did, otherwise.

And so it always came as a surprise when one of them, armed with a truly fantastic idea that ticked all of their *ikigai* boxes—something they loved, something they were good at, and something people needed and would pay for—would waste a solid week designing the perfect logo.

With all due respect for the branding and graphic designers out there (because I do think logos are important for brand clarity), these musicians didn't really need a brand (yet). They needed to build out and promote their upcoming workshop to people who already knew them, so that they could do it and get paid for it. Not a single person who would be saying *yes* to their offer cared about their logo.

It wasn't always a logo, of course. Sometimes it was business cards or a website. Or, they would spend all of their time "researching" and zero time doing anything helpful. They would alphabetize their music by composer instead of promoting their online master class, or create lists of this and lists of that, spend a whole weekend getting to Inbox Zero. There's a name for that kind of behavior: "Rocking Chair Tasks."

Rocking Chair Tasks

Rocking Chair Tasks are tasks that keep us busy, but don't lead to significant progress. They give the illusion of productivity, but don't drive goals forward. You can sit at your desk all day feeling like you're "working on your project," but at the end of the day, you're not any closer than you were that morning. Your inbox might be culled, but your project remains where it was.

"But Kate! You told us in chapter 11 to go ahead and organize our files!"

Yes, I did. And there's a reason I didn't put that information in the chapter about taking action.

If you did that organizational work back while you were reading chapter 11, then you're all set now. You can resist the Rocking Chair Tasks (sorry, no excuses!). You'll surprise yourself, though, with just how many needless, time-consuming tasks you can find to do that don't involve making progress. They often land in one of these categories:

~ Organizing (sorting, alphabetizing, creating spreadsheets)
~ Information gathering (going down search engine rabbit holes, or a social media abyss)
~ Networking (texting your friends)
~ Designing (working on logos you aren't ready to use yet)

There's a clear difference between Rocking Chair Tasks and procrastination. Procrastination is when you can't possibly get started until you clean out the basement (when your home office is on the third floor). Procrastination is an act of resisting the work that needs to get done, and it's fear-based. You are afraid you won't be able to do the work well, and so your brain convinces you to put off that horrible inevitability as long as possible. With Rocking Chair Tasks, you're a bit further along. You've recognized the procrastination for what it is and stared it down. You put the broom down, walked up from the basement to the third floor office, and sat down at your desk.

"Here we go!" you might have said to yourself, excitedly. "Let's do this!" And then, desperate for any evidence that you *can*, in fact, do this well, you reach for what seems like an easy win. But let's look at two similar tasks that have very different results. In both tasks, you take out your phone and open up your social media app of choice. In scenario 1, you create a post: "More details coming soon, but I'm excited announce my upcoming Two-Day Hip-Hop for Hippies Workshop, May 3 and 4. DM me for more info if you're interested." In scenario 2, you browse around, and "like" the posts of various people you think might be interested in your workshop. You know that this will work with the algorithm so that they will maybe see your posts more (for when you eventually announce the workshop).

See the difference? Rocking Chair Tasks aren't necessarily stupid or a complete waste of time. You're not wrong that engaging with your potential workshop participants might work in your favor algorithmically, but it hasn't actually gotten your workshop closer to existence. Whereas in scenario 1, you've let people know that it's happening, when it's happening, and what it's about. *That* post could lead to someone DM'ing you and paying for a spot in the workshop. That post moved the needle.

Needle Movers

Unlike Rocking Chair Tasks, Needle Movers are high-impact actions that directly contribute to your goals and make meaningful progress. They move the needle forward. If the Rocking Chair Task is to watch four hours of interior design YouTube videos, the Needle Mover is to fill out and send in your registration for your first interior design course. You might have gained loads of inspiration and learned a thing or two from your YouTube binge (both good things!) but you aren't actually closer to your goal of becoming an interior designer. But registering for design classes does get you closer to becoming an interior designer.

Needle Movers often (but not exclusively) fall into the following categories:

~ Writing and publishing an article
~ Sending proposals

~ Installing new software (and using it!)
~ Making a piece of art
~ Practicing a new piece
~ Setting up rehearsals
~ Booking venues/contractors/performers

It's not always the case, but Rocking Chair Tasks are very often tasks you can do that no one knows about. Needle Movers, more often than not, somehow get your work out into the world.

Exercise: Identifying Rocking Chair and Needle Mover Tasks

Identify a few tasks you've done recently and categorize them as either Rocking Chair or Needle Mover tasks. Set an intention to prioritize Needle Movers going forward.

Task:	Rocking Chair?	Needle Mover?
1.		
2.		
3.		
4.		
5.		

The Mini Leap

It can often feel very vulnerable to start working toward big new goals, resetting the dial on your potential, your identity, your relationships, everything! Even after clarifying your first three Big Goals and breaking them into smaller micro-milestones, getting yourself organized, and having your accountability partner in place, it can feel intimidating to make a start. We discussed earlier about how courage is a muscle, and maybe yours needs a bit more strength training.

That's where Mini Leaps come in. A Mini Leap will still move the needle forward, but it feels a bit easier—almost as safe as a Rocking Chair Task, although with a bit more at stake. They can help get the ball rolling, allow you to practice doing courageous acts a little at a time, strengthening that muscle bit by bit. A Mini Leap can be just the thing to start your momentum. They might look like the following:

~ Asking your next-door neighbor for the email address of their literary agent sister-in-law
~ Downloading the course registration form and filling it out
~ Booking a discovery call with a coach or trainer
~ Requesting a quote from a vendor
~ Buying new running shoes
~ Downloading the language app to your phone
~ Picking up some new art supplies

Are they easy-to-manage, low-risk tasks? Yes. Are you a teeny tiny bit closer to your goal? Also yes.

You'll sense a clear difference in how you feel after completing a Mini Leap compared to how you feel after doing a Rocking Chair Task. With the latter, you'll feel torn—tired, busy, but somehow dissatisfied. After even the smallest of Mini Leaps, you'll feel like you've done something good and worthwhile. You might even feel the urge to celebrate. And you absolutely should.

Big Jumps

Even though you'll be breaking down your goals into micro-milestones, and biting off one small piece at a time, there will inevitably be a few moments when the next step requires one Big Jump, rather than several Mini Leaps. These Big Jumps are significant actions that push you out of your comfort zone and propel your progress in a noticeable way. As you strengthen your courage muscle, taking Big Jumps will feel easier and more natural to you. Sometimes, however, they are an unavoidable and completely necessary next step. Do not pass Go. Do not collect $200 until you have made the Big Jump. Some examples of Big Jumps include:

~ Pitching to a major publication
~ Submitting the documentation for your 501(c)(3) nonprofit status
~ Showing up to your first race
~ Playing your first public concert

Taking these Big Jumps can feel nerve-racking, nausea-inducing, or nearly impossible, but afterward, you'll feel proud, exhilarated, and ready to take on the next step. These are great moments to lean on your support network. Ask your Professor for guidance. Tell your Prodder when you plan on doing it, and agree to let them know when you're finished. Plan a post-jump celebration with your Peer or your Pillar, and look to your Proof for some last-minute inspiration.

Exercise: Determining Mini Leaps and Big Jumps for Your Three Big Goals

Write down one Mini Leap and one Big Jump for each of your three Big Goals, and write in when you could take that action (for example, a Mini Leap could happen today, a Big Jump might not be called for until next month).

Goal	Mini Leap	Big Jump	When

Exercise: Self-Reflection Questions

- What does a productive, momentum-building day look like for you?
- What's one Needle Mover you can tackle today?

Momentum is the secret sauce that turns dreams into realities, and you've already taken huge steps by identifying your goals and breaking them into manageable parts. Now, as you begin to move forward, keep the difference between Rocking Chair Tasks and Needle Movers in mind, using Mini Leaps to keep your energy flowing and Big Jumps to make bold, substantial progress when the time is right.

Remember, every action counts, every Mini Leap brings you closer, and every Big Jump can transform you. Let your support network help you along the way, and don't forget to celebrate each step—big or small. Your process of becoming your Beyond Potential Self is already in motion, and each move you make is a testament to your commitment, courage, and growth.

Building a Momentum Action Plan

1. Break Down Goals into Steps: Use your micro-milestones to outline what needs to happen when. What is your first micro-milestone?

2. Differentiate Rocking Chair Tasks and Needle Movers: Avoid the first, prioritize the latter.

3. Schedule Regular Work Blocks in Your Calendar: Even if your schedule is sporadic, it's easier to move a work block than to squeeze one into a busy week.

4. Aim to Make Some Progress During Each Work Block: The ultimate momentum builder!

5. Balance Your Mini Leaps and Your Big Jumps: Build momentum without burning out.

6. Check In with Your Accountability Partner: Choose a method you can both stick to, like a weekly coffee date, a text at the end of each day to report progress, or a shared Google Doc.

7. Celebrate Your Wins: Whether they're small wins, big wins, or "learned big lessons" wins, celebrate it all.

15

Re-Ignite Your Time Management (So You Can Get to the Life Part)

Most people overestimate what they can do in a day, and underestimate what they can do in a month. We overestimate what we can do in a year, and underestimate what we can accomplish in a decade.

— Matthew Kelly

We all know that time is our most precious resource. But what we may not realize is that how we choose to *manage* our time—and how intentionally we *structure* it—can be the difference between a chaotic, burnout-ridden existence and a life that flows with purpose, productivity, and calm. This chapter is about putting a sustainable, layered time-management system in place. By planning at different levels—annual, quarterly, monthly, weekly, and daily— you can find the right time and space for your projects, keep your goals and intentions clear and actionable, minimize the stress of constant decision-making, and create a rhythm that supports both achievement and well-being.

Having a structured approach to planning isn't about rigid control; it's about giving yourself a framework that holds space for creativity, rest, and growth. Life will always throw unexpected things our way, but with a reliable system in place, we're better able to handle those bumps in the road. Let's dive in and explore how each layer of this system can work together to help you feel less overwhelmed and more in control of your time and energy.

Looking at Your Year: The Big Picture

Marketing guru Steph Crowder taught me her "Year on the Wall" system of using all twelve months of a wall calendar taped up next to one another in 2017, and I haven't looked back since. Doing my best to navigate the competing schedules of the various ensembles I played with in Boston, the chamber music program I was running, responsibilities at home, and the concerts I was setting up for myself around the world, I was desperate for a way to fit everything in without burning myself out, and this was the magical scheduling hack I was seeking.

You can decide for yourself whether you prefer to work from an academic year (September to August) or a calendar year (January to December). I stood at my blank wall calendar and a multi-color pack of mini sticky notes, and I color-coded everything that was set in stone for the year. This included my husband's school holiday weeks, weeks I had to be in Boston for rehearsals and concerts, important dates for my chamber music program, student recitals, and graduation dates. Anything I knew about went up on the calendar, and then, and only then, with an entire wall of sticky notes in front of me, could I see where things stood. December was jam-packed with holiday concerts and end-of-semester functions, but January was pretty light—that would be a great time to block off some serious practice days for my own recital repertoire, then I could schedule some concerts of that repertoire during that light week I had in February. I would be able to see that, even though I had two light weeks at the beginning of June, I would be coming off three super-intense teaching weeks, and shouldn't book a recital right then if I can help it. But it *would* be a great time to visit my family in Chicago.

This first layer of planning isn't about the details of each day, but rather a snapshot of what the year is going to look like. Where do you have some free space? When do you have time to take a vacation? What are your super-busy months? Color-coding it all allows me to make sure all the different parts of my life are somewhat balanced out over the year.

Take a few moments to think about those three Big Goals you've set for yourself. Where do those fit in? Are there months you'll be able to let them be the focus?

Tip for Flexibility: Life is unpredictable, and sometimes our plans need to evolve. Using the sticky notes instead of writing directly on the calendar pages allows you to move things around when needed. For example, one of my current goals is to host friends at our house more often. So, I went through my calendar and found one weekend night a month when we could have a dinner party. Sometimes a commitment comes up for one of the nights I had marked off, and that's fine. I can just pull off the sticky note and find a new spot for it.

Exercise: Create Your Calendar for the Year

Go through the calendars and schedules you have for your various jobs or roles. Think about your work and family calendars, kids' and students' important school events, and add them in for the upcoming twelve months. In looking at this calendar, answer the following questions:

Which months or weeks are already maxed out?

_____

Which months or weeks are a bit more spacious?

_____

How can you incorporate aspects of your three Big Goals into this calendar?

_____

_____

Breaking Your Calendar into Quarters: The 90-Day Plan

In his 2013 book, *The 12 Week Year*, author Brian Moran argued that we lose time and productivity when we give ourselves too long a runway on our goals. His book centered on the idea of setting goals in ninety-day sprints, and I completely agree. Quarterly planning bridges the gap between the big-picture vision of annual planning and the more granular focus of monthly and weekly planning. Breaking the year into quarters lets us manage our goals in more digestible chunks and make adjustments along the way.

Every three months, I schedule a Quarterly Retreat over a few days. As much as I love the idea of heading off to a cabin in the mountains to do these retreats, the reality (at least for now) is that I stay home (of course, my home is in Bermuda, so I am actually in a premium location—but that part is not a necessity). During this stay-at-home retreat, I revisit my yearly goals and assess how things are going. This is a chance to celebrate any progress, reconsider goals that no longer feel relevant, and set specific targets for the upcoming quarter.

Quarterly planning gives me the chance to prioritize areas that need more attention, pivot when necessary, and decide what I want to focus on over the next few months. I usually choose one new skill I want to improve over those ninety days. I find that three months is a long enough period to make some progress on learning a new skill, but not so long that I can justify skipping a week or two. It might be gardening, SEO, Excel, or knitting. It can be a skill that will help my work, or a skill that will enhance my life. You'd be surprised how quickly four new skills a year can add up!

Work wise, I choose one primary focus area for each quarter. For example, I might dedicate one quarter to launching a new coaching program, another to building my network, and another to travel and rejuvenation. By giving each quarter a specific *job*, I ensure that I'm moving forward with intention rather than spreading myself too thin. There are plenty of constants throughout my year, however, and it's work that I do all twelve months. But I've found that harnessing the few extra hours in each week to make sustainable progress in one specific area has far better results than trying to make progress in four areas all year round.

Exercise: Identifying Quarterly Goals

What are your main focus areas for the next quarter?

Identify one to three quarterly goals that align with your overall vision for the year.

1. _____
2. _____
3. _____

What would success look like in each area? What can you measure?

1. _____
2. _____
3. _____

What is one new skill you would like to learn or improve this quarter?

_____

_____

What should the main area of focus be for this quarter? Why?

_____

_____

Monthly Planning: Setting Focused Intentions

Monthly planning is where Big Goals start becoming tangible. It's a time to review progress on your quarterly goals, celebrate what's been working, adjust what hasn't, and set clear, focused intentions for the coming month.

At the beginning of each month, I look back at the previous month's accomplishments, challenges, and lessons learned. This gives me a chance to refine my priorities and set milestones that feel realistic and motivating. I also take a few moments to identify my Needle Movers—the key activities that will have the most impact on my goals for that month.

I like to set one to three key milestones for the month that are connected to my quarterly goals. These might include completing a specific project, reaching a download target for my podcast, or reaching a certain level of whatever new skill I chose for the quarter. Keeping those monthly milestones limited can help us stay focused and avoid burnout.

Exercise: Identifying Key Milestones for the Month

Looking at your three goals for the quarter, what can you set out to achieve in the next thirty days?

1. _____

2. _____

3. _____

What progress would you like to make on your new skill?

_____

_____

Weekly Planning: Outlining Specific Tasks

Weekly planning is about taking those monthly milestones and breaking them down into actionable steps. It's where you take the quarterly goal of "10x podcast downloads" and its corresponding monthly goal of "Hit X number of downloads" and turn it into "Find three new ways to promote the podcast." It's where you can break down the bigger *what* into the actionable *how*, prioritize what matters most, set specific tasks, and establish a realistic game plan for the week.

My weekly planning process usually happens on Sunday afternoons. I start by reviewing my monthly milestones and thinking about what needs to happen in the coming week to keep me on track, and then write out a master list of everything that needs to happen in each area. Then, I prioritize tasks that will move the needle on my goals, and schedule them into my calendar. When I wake up on Monday morning, everything has an assigned spot for when I will work on them.

There are two mistakes I see people making at this level. The first: They'll make that master to-do list, and wake up on Monday morning with a blank calendar and a big to-do list. Feeling like there's plenty of time to get it all done, they're in no hurry. They procrastinate during the first half of the week, and then are in a sudden panic when they realize it's already Thursday and they haven't gained any traction. This is usually the day your friend texts you that they're in town and would love to meet up. Of course you want to see them, but now you're even further behind.

The second mistake that people make is that they'll look at their master list and charge through it from top to bottom without prioritizing actions or looking for the Needle Movers. By Thursday, they're exhausted from picking up the dry cleaning and sending those quick, inconsequential emails, making doctor's appointments, and so on. But they've still made zero progress toward their bigger goals. They ran out of steam before they got that far.

To avoid both of those mistakes, make sure you're doing two things:

1. Give every task a spot on the calendar. Monday, from 10:00 to 11:00 a.m., you're going to email these four people. Wednesday, from 9:00 a.m. to 12:00 p.m, you're going to write a draft of the grant proposal, etc. You can move things around (like when your friend shows up from out of town) but at least you know how big a block you need to find.

2. Try to complete at least one needle-moving task each day: It can be a small task or a big one, but if you can end each day pointing to one way that you are closer to your goal, you'll feel like a million bucks. (It's that dopamine, again.)

To make weekly planning easier, I sometimes assign themes to my days, like Admin Mondays, Writing Wednesdays, or PR Fridays. This structure helps reduce decision fatigue and gives each day a purpose. It's not often I have the luxury of dedicating an entire day to one theme, but going into each week, I'll tend to put any administrative tasks on Monday, plan to do any writing projects (an article, podcast script, etc.) on Wednesday, and schedule interviews for Fridays. Once you get into the habit of doing this, it becomes second nature. And your brain (and your nervous system!) will thank you.

Exercise: Identifying Priorities and Deadlines to Create Themes

My top three priorities for this coming week are:

1. _____

2. _____

3. _____

Approaching deadlines include:

1. _____

2. _____

3. _____

My daily themes could be:

Monday: _____

Tuesday: _____

Wednesday: _____

Thursday: _____

Friday: _____

Saturday: _____

Sunday: _____

Make sure you set aside time for reflection at the end of the week to review what went well, what didn't, and what adjustments you might need for next week.

Daily Planning: Building an Actionable Routine

Daily planning helps you stay focused on what needs to be done each day without feeling overwhelmed. It's the final layer of your time-management system, where you set intentions, prioritize tasks, and build a routine that supports productivity and peace.

Because I scheduled my weekly to-do list into each day, my approach to my daily routine is pretty simple. I just show up and do what I said I'd do. I already have an idea of what my needle-moving tasks are, and know how great it's going to feel to get those done.

The biggest obstacles I face in my daily routine have nothing to do with not knowing *what* to do, but with managing my time and energy. I might be less enthusiastic about the day's plan if I didn't sleep well the night before, for example. Two strategies I use to manage this are Time-Blocking and the Pomodoro Technique.

Time-Blocking

Time-blocking is when you dedicate specific blocks of time to particular tasks or types of work. This helps you create focused sessions that reduce distractions and improve efficiency. For instance, if you take a look at that giant to-to list you created for the week, you might have a bunch of unrelated emails to send. One is to your kid's teacher, another is about the gig you have next month, and then you need to email the airline about a reimbursement, etc. These are all small, random, easy-to-forget to-do items. By blocking off one hour on Monday mornings from eight to nine, you can sit down and knock them all out. You're right there at the computer, pulling up contact information and getting things done like some kind of email ninja. Bam! You just wiped out eight things from your list at once. Likewise, if you know you have to learn a stack of new music for some upcoming rehearsals, block off a certain amount of time for that practice. There is a huge difference between "I'm going to practice when I get home tonight" and "I'm going to practice from six to eight tonight."

"When I get home tonight" could get pushed off later and later if your colleagues want to meet after work, or you decide to stop at the grocery store on the way home, or any number of ways you could get delayed. Before you know it, it's seven thirty by the time you're walking in the door. You haven't even started cooking dinner, so forget practicing! The latter, time-blocked session makes it a *choice*. You need to be home by six so that you can practice from six to eight. If your colleagues want to meet up after work, you can make that decision. "Am I willing to practice from seven to nine instead?" The block can move, but it still needs to happen. If you're fine with it, great. If not, you can take a pass on the work hangout and get yourself home.

For me, time-blocking is essential. I reserve blocks of time for deep work, where I focus entirely on one project or task without interruption. I also set aside time for meetings, personal projects, and breaks, making sure that each part of my day has a clear purpose. By assigning certain hours to specific types of tasks, I avoid the mental exhaustion that comes from constantly switching between activities, and have everything I need for that kind of task.

Exercise: Creating a Weekly Time-Blocking Schedule

Try creating your own weekly time-blocking schedule. Map out your main work hours, and assign blocks for key activities. Include deep work blocks, meeting times, and personal or break periods. Once your schedule is set, give yourself a week to try it out, making adjustments as needed to fit your own personal rhythm.

Tip: To make time-blocking work, it's important to avoid interruptions during these focused sessions. I use alarms to mark the end of each time block and set clear boundaries with others so they know when I'm unavailable. When I'm in a deep-work block, I disable notifications on my devices and go into "Do not disturb" mode.

The Pomodoro Technique

The Pomodoro Technique is a time-management strategy that involves working in short, focused intervals (usually twenty-five minutes), followed by a brief break. These work sprints, called "Pomodoros," can help maintain concentration and reduce fatigue.

Research suggests that short work sessions followed by breaks can improve focus and prevent burnout. The technique helps you make the most of your energy without overwhelming yourself, especially during demanding or repetitive tasks. It's quite easy for me to get into such a steady rhythm of working that I won't move or get up for hours on end. The result is that, while I did get quite a lot done in that period, it's exhausting, and my brain feels foggy the rest of the day. When I force myself to take a five-minute break every twenty-five minutes, I'm able to get far more work done in the long run. I maintain my energy, and stepping away and coming back to the work keeps the perspective fresh.

You'll also find that when you're staring down what feels like a huge, intimidating task, knowing that you *only* need to work on it for twenty-five minutes makes it seem far more manageable. You can do anything for twenty-five minutes. Every time I've found myself in this situation, I've found that once I get through that first sprint, I'm excited to come back for more after my five-minute break.

Bonus: You'd be amazed what you can accomplish in those five minutes. Fold some of that laundry, put the dishes away, water the houseplants, text a friend, drink a glass of water, do some push-ups. Those, too, add up throughout the day and you'll find that you are getting more done in all areas of your life.

Exercise: Your Pomodoro Day

Try a Pomodoro Day where you use a timer to complete four Pomodoro sessions, with short breaks in-between. Check in on how you feel at the end of the day—did the breaks improve your focus? Did the timed sprints make tasks feel more manageable?

Incorporating Self-Care to Prevent Burnout

If you're reading this book, you're probably a bit of a high achiever. You've worked hard your entire life, and discipline and sacrifice are in your DNA. I would be doing you a disservice, however, if a chapter on time management didn't include a word about scheduling in rest and play, as well. Self-care is not just a personal indulgence; it's an essential part of a sustainable productivity system. Downtime, hobbies, and rest are crucial to your long-term success and mental well-being, preventing the burnout that so many creatives face. When you think back to your Beyond Potential Self, was that image of a miserable, burned-out workaholic? No, I didn't think so. Nobody strives for that.

My clients hear me talk a lot about "scheduling in the pink." For my color-coded life, social engagements or time off is always designated in pink. Lunch with a friend on Wednesday? That's in pink. Sunday Night Quiz? Pink. Dinner with friends on Friday? Pink. You can, of course, choose whatever color you want for your fun, but when you look over your week, you should see it sprinkled in here and there.

Days Off: To incorporate self-care into my routine, I schedule buffer days for rest and make time for hobbies that recharge me—like gardening. I also set aside specific blocks of time each week reserved solely for nonwork activities. This isn't always an easy thing to do for creatives with inconsistent schedules, but more often than not, you know what the week or two ahead look like. See where you can block off time. You don't need to work seven days a week. There's no prize at the end for the person who had the fewest days off in their life. In fact, your Beyond Potential Self would find that pretty sad.

Exercise: Identifying Personal Activities

List ten personal activities that recharge you, whether it's reading, walking, or spending time with friends. Treat these activities as essential appointments with yourself, giving them the same respect as your work commitments. Try to schedule at least two to three of them into every week.

1. _____

2. _____

3. _____

4. _____

5. _____

6. _____

7. _____

8. _____

9. _____

10. _____

Conclusion: Bringing It All Together

As we wrap up this chapter, I hope you see how each layer of this time-management system can support a more balanced, fulfilling, and sustainable approach to work and life. Yearly, quarterly, monthly, weekly, and daily planning each serve a unique purpose, helping you keep your vision and goals clear, and your actions focused. Time-blocking and the Pomodoro Technique provide structure within each day, while prioritizing rest and time for fun help you maintain momentum without burning out. While on paper, all of this *scheduling* (as opposed to the *doing*) can seem like a waste of time, you'll find that the more consistently you do them, the more automatic they become, and the less time they take.

How could these strategies fit into your own life? Which level of planning feels most comfortable? Which technique would have the biggest impact on your routine? Take time to experiment and find what works best for you. Remember, *consistency is key*. By building these methods into your life and making them a habit, you'll be able to make meaningful progress toward your goals without sacrificing your well-being.

And as you move forward, don't forget to celebrate the wins, big and small—we'll be covering that more in the next chapter. Every step is progress, and every accomplishment is a reminder that you're building a life and career that you love—one intentional step at a time.

16

Re-Ignite Your Joy: Celebrating Your New Self

The more you praise and celebrate your life, the more there is in life to celebrate.

– Oprah Winfrey

Why Celebration Matters

Growing up in the classical music world, your fiercest competitors were also your best friends. For every audition, competition, or orchestra seating challenge, one of you was going to end the day very happy, and the rest were not. We learned very quickly to accept our win with grace (and barely a smile), and then turn our attention to consoling our friends and telling them how wonderful they sounded. It's a beautiful thing. We were taught from that young age to be mindful of the feelings of others even as we experienced a win. But it also set a poor precedent—that you shouldn't celebrate your own achievements. Instead, you should remain humble and quiet about any success. Anything else would be considered bragging.

This is the way things work in many facets of the arts world. You would never go up to your colleagues and say, "Guess what! I just won a huge award!" And sadly, those same colleagues will likely be pretty quiet about it too—even if it's public knowledge. There's a pervading sense that we do what we do, not for the external rewards and recognition, but for the passion we have for the art.

I think both can coexist, and also that the world of the arts, and the lives of the artists within it, would be vastly improved if we were a little better at celebrating.

When we think of celebration, our minds often jump to grand gestures or milestone achievements, but celebration is more than that. It's a tool for reinforcing the positive changes we're working so hard to create. Celebration helps us pause, acknowledge progress, and show gratitude for the process itself. It's a way to honor the growth that often happens quietly, in small, almost imperceptible steps, and to nurture the resilience that keeps us moving forward.

In this final chapter, we'll explore how to embrace celebration as a meaningful, ongoing practice. Whether it's recognizing a small internal shift or a major external result, these moments of acknowledgment fuel our motivation and encourage us to keep going. Celebrating doesn't just mark an end point; it creates momentum, strengthens our sense of purpose, and helps us build a joyful and sustainable path forward. It helps reinforce that we are on the right path—heading toward our Beyond Potential Self.

Acknowledging the Small Wins Along the Way

Big Goals are often built on small wins, and recognizing these incremental achievements is essential. Psychologist Teresa Amabile's and researcher/writer Steven Kramer's research[2] on the power of small wins showed that even modest progress can have a significant impact on motivation and happiness. These little acknowledgments help break up what might otherwise feel like an overwhelming journey, especially when major milestones still feel far off.

The first time I experienced this was when I was in my first small-group coaching cohort. Every Friday, we were encouraged to name our wins for the week in the private Facebook group. At first, this felt horribly awkward. Some of the small wins I had accumulated over the week felt silly and insignificant, and when listing the big win, I heard those thoughts rattling around my brain: "Nobody likes a bragger, Kate!" But as I contemplated what to do, I could see my co-participants adding in their wins—small ones, big ones. And, knowing what they were working on, I was happy for each and every one of them. I knew how hard they were working, and also knew firsthand how good it felt to accomplish each of those things. Emojis of support were flying around, and finally, I felt okay about adding in my own.

The support I felt regarding my own wins was palpable. With every heart and like and dancing girl emoji, it felt like we were having a mini celebration. I was on cloud nine, and I was also seriously motivated to continue that streak. I couldn't wait to see what wins I'd be listing the following Friday, and the one after that.

Think about a recent project or goal you've been working on. Maybe it's learning a new quarterly skill, finishing a chapter of a book, or making progress on another major project. These small steps forward are all victories worth celebrating. Consider setting aside a few moments each day to reflect on one thing that went well. Perhaps you kept a positive mindset during a tough moment, completed a small task, or simply stayed committed to the work.

---

2 Teresa Amabile and Steven Kramer, "The Power of Small Wins," Harvard Business Review, May 2011, https://hbr.org/2011/05/the-power-of-small-wins

---

Exercise: Making a Habit out of Celebrating

Daily Reflection: At the end of each day, jot down one small victory. These can be as simple as "I showed up" or "I finished that task I was avoiding." Over time, you'll start to notice a list of wins, reinforcing the progress you're making.

Mini Celebrations: Treat yourself to small rewards—perhaps a favorite snack, a quick walk, or a few minutes to enjoy a hobby—whenever you reach a minor milestone.

Celebrating Failure

Growth isn't always about winning. Our greatest leaps often come from moments of struggle and failure. Learning to celebrate these times of growth is a way of honoring our courage. Reframing failure as a learning opportunity not only fosters self-compassion, but also strengthens our resolve to continue.

When I was working with performance coach Dr. Don Greene at the New World Symphony in Miami, he was adamant that any time we took an audition, we had to get ourselves a gift. It didn't have to be expensive, and it couldn't be anything to be consumed. It had to remain with us so we could see it and be reminded of that specific audition—whether the audition was good or bad. I still have a stuffed Beanie Baby gorilla I bought at the Houston airport after auditioning for the Symphony there. I hadn't properly prepared, and I spent more time hanging out with my friends and hosts than I did practicing while I was there. Of course, I didn't play well. And to this day, that gorilla reminds me of that lesson. Celebrating that realization was an important moment for me, and allowed me to have much better success in the future. And doing it by buying myself a gift was much kinder than beating myself up about it mentally.

Instead of seeing setbacks as clear and certain evidence of inadequacy, we can choose to view them as necessary steps on the path to reaching our goals. Celebrating these moments reminds us that growth is rarely linear and that the process of learning and adapting according to our results is worth a win in itself.

Exercise: Reframing Past Failures

Name a time that you *failed* at something:

_____

What lessons did you learn from that experience?

_____

_____

What successes has that new knowledge led to?

_____

_____

How can you take a moment to celebrate that past failure as a moment of growth?

_____

_____

Celebrating with the People You Love

Celebrations are often more joyful when shared. When we invite others into our wins—whether big or small—we create a sense of community and connection that enriches our lives and reinforces our progress. Sharing celebrations with family, friends, or colleagues can also make our achievements feel more real.

Inviting others into our process can deepen relationships, build a feeling of camaraderie, and even provide additional support for the goals we're striving toward. Whether you're going out for a quiet dinner with close friends, having a virtual toast with faraway family members, or running out to get an ice cream cone with your partner, celebrating together is a way of saying, "We're in this together."

The key word here, however, is "inviting." It's important that the person who experiences the win has a say in how it's celebrated. I had a client a few years ago who pulled off an impressive two-week online event. When she logged off for the final time, her family was nowhere to be found. They had left the house to give her some space, but that left her feeling extremely alone in that big moment. She said, "I felt like I had just won a gold medal, but no one cared enough to be there to congratulate me." The next year, in the days leading up to the close of the event, she told her family what she needed. She wanted to be immediately surrounded by the people she loved to smile and shriek, and whoop and holler, and celebrate both her massive achievement and the fact that she was done. And on that last day, after she logged off for the final time, her family was there waiting with flowers, and signs, and a picnic lunch. It was exactly what she wanted and needed.

The truth is that no matter how well we think people know us, they cannot know exactly how we will want to celebrate something. It's the spouse who throws the big surprise party when all the birthday boy wanted was a quiet steak dinner á deux (or vice versa). It can be hard to ask for these things, but it's still important to do so. It will also encourage your loved ones to let *you* know how *they* want to be celebrated when it's their turn.

Exercise: Your Celebration Style

Think of something you're working on that you'll want to celebrate. What would feel special to you? If you could plan your celebration, what would it include?

Now, be sure to share this idea with the people or person you'd want to celebrate with.

Celebrating by Yourself

Sometimes, the most powerful celebrations are the quiet, personal ones. Solo celebrations allow us to honor our achievements without external validation. They're a reminder that our progress and efforts matter, even if no one else is around to witness them.

Personal celebration can take many forms—a peaceful walk in nature, a favorite meal, a trip to the spa, or simply a moment of gratitude. Whatever feels special and restorative to you can be a way to celebrate.

Exercise: Personalizing Your Celebrations

- Self-Celebration Ritual: Identify a small ritual you can do just for yourself whenever you accomplish something meaningful. It might be as simple as taking a few quiet minutes to breathe and acknowledge your progress, getting yourself a scoop of your favorite ice cream, or making a large bowl of popcorn and watching *Love, Actually* for the millionth time (no one's judging). The key is to make it personal and intentional.

- Send Yourself a Card: Think of something you've done in your life that you're proud of. It can be an accomplishment, a decision, a learned skill, etc. Select a nice card, and then write yourself a congratulatory note. Say all the things you'd like to hear. You can mention how hard you worked, or how proud you are of listening to your intuition, or how relieved you must feel for it to be over. Say it all. Then address it to yourself and send it in the mail to yourself. Trust me on this one.

Celebrating with a Team

In team settings, celebrating accomplishments is about building a culture of acknowledgment. When teams celebrate wins together, it fosters unity, reinforces shared goals, and can boost morale and productivity. Celebrations don't have to be grand—they can be simple acknowledgments that say, "Your efforts matter."

In creative fields, the idea of a team can be anything from your small, newly formed dance company to your studio full of elementary school piano students. It might be a board that you're chairing, or group of artist friends you gathered to create a show. All that is required is two or more people who worked toward a common goal.

Creating a team culture that values celebration can have lasting impacts on both individual and collective performance. When team members feel seen and appreciated, they're more likely to remain engaged, committed, and motivated to keep pushing toward shared objectives. You'll find that food often comes in handy for creating such a culture. In my orchestra, for instance, bringing some snacks and drinks to each rehearsal went a long way in getting people to chat and get to know each other better. Friendships deepened, and everyone felt like they were part of the same team, rather than a single player who showed up to rehearsal, did their part, and headed home.

Exercise: Team Celebrations

One important team I am a part of right now is:

_____

A goal we are working toward that we could celebrate is:

_____

One idea for celebrating together might be:

_____

Embracing Celebration as an Ongoing Practice

Celebration isn't a luxury or a reward to be reserved only for big achievements; it's a practice that fuels joy, courage, and sustained motivation. As you move forward toward your goals and your vision of your Beyond Potential Self, remember that each small step is a piece of the larger process, and every moment of growth is worth recognizing. Building celebration into your routine is a way of saying to yourself, "Doing this is a big deal. And this journey is worth savoring."

Think about ways you can build regular celebration into your life. List small ways to mark wins, both solo and shared, and commit to incorporating these moments of joy and gratitude into your path forward.

Celebrating your new self isn't just about marking where you've been; it's about nurturing the joy, purpose, and fulfillment that will carry you into the future.

Final Thoughts

One of my most-read articles is a piece I wrote called "The $100 Bill." It's the story of one of my young students who came into his weekly cello lesson wanting to improve his sound. Week after week, we would go over what he needed to do; he would show me that he could do it—that he understood it all very clearly. He would leave his lesson, full of excitement about his new resonant sound, only to return the next week with the same dilemma, and we'd do the same thing all over again.

It was as if he were telling me he wanted to buy a certain toy, but needed $100 for it. I would show him a crisp $100 bill sitting by the door—it was his to take and he could buy his toy—and week after week, he would walk out the door, leaving that crisp $100 bill right where it was.

Hearing this metaphor, he realized he needed to take what we did in the lesson home with him, and *actually* work on it each day. It wasn't enough to *know* how to make a great sound; he needed to actively practice it in order for it to become a part of him.

It's one thing to acquire knowledge about how to solve our problems or reach new heights, but it's *what we do* with that knowledge that makes all the difference. We all know exactly what we need to do—whether it's about learning Spanish, or training for a half-marathon, or writing that screenplay. Some will do it and will slowly but surely become their Beyond Potential Self. Others will wait until tomorrow, or the next day, or the next. And when they finally are confronted by that ideal version of who they could have been, they'll be left wondering why they didn't just start. Why did they let their life slip away from them?

Through the pages of this book, you have broken apart your past, dug deep into why your current life looks the way it does—the good parts and those you'd like to change. You've learned to reframe your thinking and see possibilities where none existed before. You got honest with yourself about what it is you truly want to do with your one, beautiful life—and why you want it. And then I've shown you how to do it. You've learned how to break it down into manageable bites, map it out, and start doing it one step at a time and in the right direction.

As a fellow creative who has gone through this process before you (and continues to go through this process alongside you), I promise: It's worth the effort. You have so much to give this world, and we're counting on you to be exactly who you truly are in order to give it.

Consider this book your $100 bill to get you started. Take it, and start creating your most true, Beyond Potential life.

Acknowledgments

Writing a book is a mostly solitary pursuit, but getting a book out into the world truly takes a village. I would like to show my sincere gratitude to my village: Jeniffer Thompson and the team over at Monkey C Media for their expert guidance and infinite patience. My editor, Nancy Daniels who was the very first person I trusted with these words from my heart—it was a good choice. Susan Blackwell and Laura Camien, and my entire cohort of Illume co-conspirators. Would this book have even been written without you guys? Not sure. Tara Mohr, whose own brilliance taught me how to coach, how to love more fully, and most importantly, how to live Beyond my Potential and Play Bigger. My incredible clients, who have trusted me (and you) with their stories and their lives—working with you has been an absolute honor and privilege. My amazing friends—Renée, Sarah, Sandy, Julie, and Vanessa—for cheering me on through the emotional rollercoaster of writing a book, for reading chapters, giving feedback, and for promising to buy a copy. I'm holding you all to it!

And finally, an enormous thank you to my husband Paul—my love, my rock, and my absolute hero. thank you for taking on the extra dog walks, cooking of meals, and household chores, and for giving me all the space and support to write (and not asking me a million questions about it!). I know you won't ever read this book because it doesn't have enough pictures in it, but I couldn't have done it without you.

Photo Credit: Nolwenn Pugi

About the Author

Kate Kayaian is a career and mindset coach for artists and creatives. She runs her signature group program, The Creatives Leadership Academy, and maintains a small roster of one-to-one clients. Kate started her podcast, *Tales from The Lane* in 2023 as a career and lifestyle-focused resource geared toward creative entrepreneurs. *Beyond Potential* is her first full-length book.

A former professional cellist, she attended the prestigious New England Conservatory of Music and went on to have a thriving career—performing with several Grammy Award-winning groups and touring as a solo and chamber musician. When the pandemic hit in early 2020, she pivoted to the online space, and she's never looked back.

She lives on the beautiful island of Bermuda with her husband and rescue pup and spends her days working with clients, writing, gardening, and serving on several nonprofit boards. She believes that everyone has the right to live exactly the kind of life they have always dreamed of living.

Learn more about Kate on her website: KateKayaian.com
Follow Kate on Instagram: @kkayaian
Free Guide! 10 Habits of Successful Artists:
　　　https://mailchi.mp/b97d167bd642/10habits

Connect with Kate

To learn more about Kate Kayaian, access resources to support your creative journey, or inquire about booking her as a speaker, workshop facilitator, or coach, head to **KateKayaian.com**.

Follow Kate on **Instagram at @kkayaian** for insights, inspiration, and a closer look at her work helping artists re-define success and re-ignite their passion for creativity.

Get Kate's free resources to elevate your artistic career today!

- ~ **10 Habits of Successful Artists**: Discover the strategies successful artists use to thrive creatively and professionally.
- ~ **Quarterly Retreat Planning Guide**: Plan intentional and productive work retreats that help you refocus and achieve your goals, 90 Days at a time.

Get them here: KateKayaian.com/BPresources